A GUIDE TO CRYPTOCURRENCY, INVESTING IN BITCOIN

BITCOIN -
The Future of
Money

I0500238

$100 Billion

This book will help you understand what bitcoin is all about and show you how this will transform the way you do business in the 21st Century!!!

Dr. G Chopra
June 2017

Table of Contents

Notes :

Design

The block chain

The *block chain* is a public **ledger** that records bitcoin transactions. A novel solution accomplishes this without any trusted central authority: maintenance of the block chain is performed by a **network** of communicating **nodes** running bitcoin software.[14] Transactions of the form *payer X sends Y bitcoins to payee Z* are broadcast to this network using readily available software applications. Network nodes can validate transactions, add them to their copy of the ledger, and then broadcast these ledger additions to other nodes.[10] The block chain is a **distributed**. database; in order to independently verify the chain of ownership of any and every bitcoin (amount), each network node stores its own copy of the block chain. Approximately six times per hour, a new group of accepted transactions, a block, is created, added to the block chain, and quickly published to all nodes.

Bitcoin		
bitcoin		
Prevailing bitcoin logo		
ISO 4217		
Code	XBT[a]	
Denominations		
Subunit		
10^{-3}	millibitcoin[1]	
10^{-6}	microbitcoin, bit[9]	
10^{-8}	satoshi[10]	
Symbol	BTC,[note 1] XBT,[note 2] **B** (B)[note 3]	
millibitcoin[1]	mBTC	
microbitcoin, bit[9]	µBTC	
Coins	Unspent outputs of transactions denominated in any multiple of satoshis[8]:ch. 5	
Demographics		
Date of introduction	3 January 2009; 8 years ago	
User(s)	Worldwide	
Issuance		
Administration	Decentralized[11][12]	
Valuation		
Supply growth	12.5 bitcoins per block (approximately every ten minutes) until mid 2020,[13] and then afterwards 6.25 bitcoins per block for 4 years until next halving. This halving continues until 2110–40, when 21 million bitcoins will have been issued.	

This allows bitcoin software to determine when a particular bitcoin amount has been spent, which is necessary in order to prevent **double-spending** in an environment without central oversight. Whereas a conventional ledger records the transfers of actual **bills** or **promissory notes** that exist apart from it, the block chain is the only place that bitcoins can be said to exist in the form of unspent outputs of transactions.[10]

Units

The unit of account of the bitcoin system is bitcoin. As of 2014, symbols used to represent bitcoin are BTC,[note 2] XBT,[note 3] and **₿**.[note 4][34]:1 Small multiples of bitcoin used as alternative units are millibitcoin (mBTC), microbitcoin (μBTC), and satoshi. Named in homage to bitcoin's creator, a *satoshi* is the smallest multiple of bitcoin representing 0.00000001 bitcoin, which is one hundred millionth of a bitcoin.[4] A *millibitcoin* equals to 0.001 bitcoin, which is one thousandth of bitcoin.[10] One *microbitcoin* equals to 0.000001 bitcoin, which is one millionth of bitcoin. A microbitcoin is sometimes referred to as a *bit*.

On 7 October 2014, the **Bitcoin Foundation** revealed a plan to apply for an ISO 4217 currency code for bitcoin,[5] and mentioned BTC and XBT as the leading candidates.[35]

Ownership

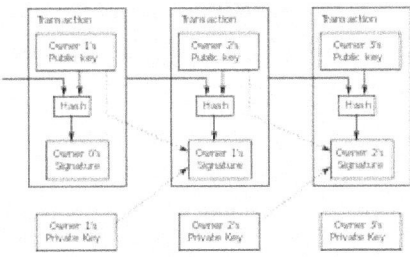

Simplified chain of ownership.[12] In reality, a transaction can have more than one input and more than one output.

Ownership of bitcoins implies that a user can spend bitcoins associated with a specific address. To do so, a payer must **digitally sign** the transaction using the corresponding **private key**. Without knowledge of the private key the transaction cannot be signed and bitcoins cannot be spent. The network verifies the signature using the **public key**.[10] If the private key is lost, the **bitcoin network** will not recognize any other evidence of ownership;[14] the coins are then lost and cannot be recovered. For example, in 2013 one user said he lost 7,500 bitcoins, worth $7.5 million at the time, when he discarded a hard drive containing his private key.[36]

Transactions

See also: Bitcoin network

A transaction must have one or more inputs. For the transaction to be valid, every input must be an unspent output of a previous transaction. Every input must be digitally signed. The use of multiple inputs corresponds to the use of multiple coins in a cash transaction. A transaction can also have multiple outputs, allowing one to make multiple payments in one go. A transaction output can be specified as an arbitrary multiple of satoshi. Similarly as in a cash transaction, the sum of inputs (coins used to pay) can exceed the intended sum of payments. In such case, an additional output is used, returning the change back to the payer.[10]

To send money to a bitcoin address, users can click links on webpages; this is accomplished with a provisional Bitcoin URI scheme using a template registered with IANA. Bitcoin clients like Electrum and Armory (software) support Bitcoin URIs. Mobile clients recognize Bitcoin URIs in QR codes, so that the user does not have to type the bitcoin address and amount in manually. The QR code is generated from the user input based on the payment amount. The QR code is displayed on the mobile device screen and can be scanned by a second mobile device.[37]

Mining

See also: Cryptographic nonce and Proof of work

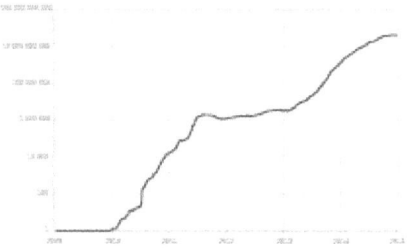

Relative mining difficulty[note 9]chart.[note 10] Vertical axis: relative mining difficulty, the scale islogarithmic. Horizontal axis: date ranging from 2009-01-09 to 2014-12-31.

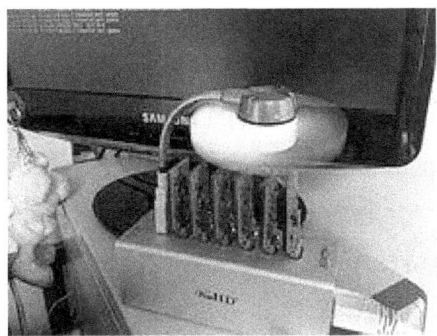

Obsolete bitcoin mining hardware called ASICMiner Block Erupter USB common in mid and late 2013.[note 11]

Mining is a record-keeping service.[note 12] Miners keep the block chain consistent, complete, and unalterable by repeatedly verifying and collecting newly broadcast transactions into a new group of transactions called a *block*. A new block contains information that "chains" it to the previous block thus giving the block chain its name. It is a **cryptographic hash** of the previous block, using the **SHA-256** hashing algorithm.[40]

A new block must also contain a so-called *proof-of-work*. The proof-of-work consists of a number called a *difficulty target* and a number called a *nonce*, which is **jargon** for "a number used only once". Miners have to find a nonce that yields a hash of the new block numerically smaller than the number provided in the difficulty target. When the new block is created and distributed to the network, every network node can easily verify the proof.[10] On the other hand, finding the proof requires significant work since for a secure cryptographic hash there is only one method to find the requisite nonce: miners try different integer values one at a time, e.g., 1, then 2, then 3, and so on until the requisite output is obtained. The fact that the hash of the new block is smaller than the difficulty target serves as a proof that this tedious work has been done, hence the name "proof-of-work".

By changing the difficulty target number, the average time required to find a nonce can be shortened or extended (A smaller number reduces the range of accepted nonces and increases the time required.) The bitcoin system adjusts the difficulty target number every 2016 blocks so that the average time the entire network needs to find a nonce always remains about ten minutes. In this way the bitcoin protocol ensures that it will always take about ten minutes to add a new block regardless of the size of the network or the sophistication of the mining hardware it employs.[10] For example, at the end of April 2014 miners had to try 34.4 quintillion values at average before finding the requisite nonce, while at the end of October 2014 it was 154.6 quintillion values at average.

The proof-of-work system alongside the chaining of blocks makes modifications of the block chain extremely hard as an attacker must modify all subsequent blocks in order for modifications of one block to be accepted. As new blocks are mined all the time, the difficulty of modifying a block increases as time passes and the number of subsequent blocks increases.[41]

Environmental costs

The environmental costs of mining include first and foremost electricity cost. Even if all miners used energy efficient processes, the combined electricity consumption would be 1.46 terawatt-h per year, equal to the consumption of about 135,000 American homes.[42] It has been estimated that the annual environmental impact due to bitcoin mining represents approximately 0.13% of the amount of impact created by fiat and gold-based monetary systems.[43]

Mining pools

As of 2014, it has become common for miners to join organized mining pools,[44] which are used primarily to reduce variance.[45]A pool splits the work among its members and has a much larger chance to win the reward. The reward is then split among the members creating a more steady stream of income without necessarily lowering the total expected amount of rewards for each miner when averaged over time, although a fee may be charged for the service.[46][47] Even for those who join pools, the cost of the electricity necessary to mine may outweigh the rewards from doing so.[48]

Supply

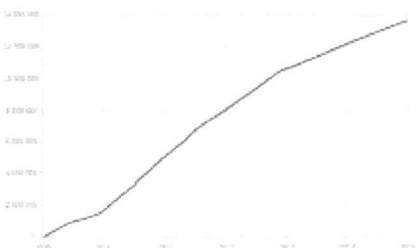

Total bitcoins in circulation.[note 10]Horizontal axis: date ranging from 2009-01-09 to 2014-12-31.

The successful miner finding the new block is rewarded with newly created bitcoins and transaction fees.[49] As of 28 November 2012,[50] the reward amounts to 25 newly created bitcoins per block added to the block chain. To claim the reward, a special transaction called a *coinbase* is included with the processed payments.[10] All bitcoins in circulation can be traced back to such coinbase transactions. The bitcoin protocolspecifies that the reward for adding a block will be halved approximately every four years. Eventually, the reward will be removed entirely when an arbitrary limit of 21 million bitcoins is reached c. 2140, and record keeping will then be rewarded by transaction fees solely.[51]

Transaction fees

Paying a transaction fee is optional, but may speed up confirmation of the transaction.[52] Payers have an incentive to include such fees because doing so means their transaction will likely be added to the block chain sooner; miners can choose which transactions to process[25] and prioritize those that pay fees. Fees are based on the storage size of the transaction generated, which in turn is dependent on the number of inputs used to create the transaction. Furthermore, priority is given to older unspent inputs.[53]

Wallets

See also: Digital wallet and Armory (software)

Electrum bitcoin wallet

Bitcoin paper wallet generated at bitaddress.org

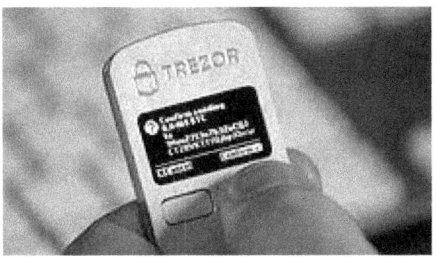

Trezor hardware wallet

A *wallet* stores the information necessary to transact bitcoins. While wallets are often described as a place to hold[54] or store bitcoins,[55] due to the nature of the system, bitcoins are inseparable from the block chain transaction ledger. Perhaps a better way to describe a wallet is something that "stores the digital credentials for your bitcoin holdings"[55] and "allows you to access (and spend) them". Bitcoin uses **public-key cryptography**, in which two cryptographic keys, one public and one private, are generated.[56] At its most basic, a wallet is a collection of these keys.

There are several types of wallets. *Software wallets* connect to the network and allow spending bitcoins in addition to holding the credentials that prove ownership.[57] Internet services called *online wallets* like Blockchain.info, Circle, or Coinbase offer similar functionality but may be easier to use.[58] *Physical wallets* also exist and are more secure, as they store the credentials necessary to spend bitcoins offline.[55] Examples combine a novelty coin with these credentials printed on metal,[59] wood, or plastic. Others are simply paper printouts. Another type of wallet called a *hardware wallet* keeps credentials offline while facilitating transactions.[60]

Reference implementation

The first wallet program, called Bitcoin-Qt, was released in 2009 by Satoshi Nakamotoas open-source code.[57] It can be used as a desktop wallet for payments or as a server utility for merchants and other payment services. Bitcoin-Qt, also called Satoshi client, is sometimes referred to as the **reference client** because it serves to define the bitcoin protocol and acts as a standard for other implementations.[57] As of version 0.9, Bitcoin-Qt has been renamed Bitcoin Core to avoid confusion.[61]

Privacy

Privacy is achieved by not identifying owners of bitcoin addresses while making other transaction data public. Bitcoin users are not identified by name, but transactions can be linked to individuals and companies.[62] Additionally, bitcoin exchanges, where people buy and sell bitcoins for fiat money, may be required by law to collect personal information.[63] To maintain financial privacy, a different bitcoin address for each transaction is recommended.[64] Transactions that spend coins from multiple inputs can reveal that the inputs may have a common owner. Users concerned about privacy can use so-called mixing services that swap coins they own for coins with different transaction histories.[65] It has been suggested that bitcoin payments should not be considered more private than cr: card payments.[66]

Fungibility

Wallets and similar software technically handle bitcoins as equivalent, establishing the basic level of **fungibility**. Researchers have pointed out that the history of every single bitcoin is registered and publicly available in the block chain ledger, and that some users may refuse to accept bitcoins coming from controversial transactions, which would harm bitcoin's fungibility.[67][better source needed] Projects such as Zerocoin and Dark Wallet aim to address these privacy and fungibility issues.[68][69]

History

Main article: History of bitcoin

Bitcoin was invented by Satoshi Nakamoto,[note 6] who published his invention on 31 October 2008 in a research paper called "Bitcoin: A Peer-to-Peer Electronic Cash system".[12] It was implemented as **open source code** and released in January 2009. Bitcoin is often called the first **cryptocurrency**[19] although prior proposals existed.[note 8] Bitcoin is more correctly described as the first decentralized **digital currency**.[14][22]

One of the first supporters, adopters, contributor to bitcoin and receiver of the first bitcoin transaction was programmer **Hal Finney**. Finney downloaded the bitcoin software the day it was released, and received 10 bitcoins from Nakamoto in the world's first bitcoin transaction.[70][71]

Other early supporters were Wei Dai, creator of bitcoin predecessor *b-money*, and Nick Szabo, creator of bitcoin predecessor *bit gold*.[72]

In 2010, an **exploit** in an early bitcoin client was found that allowed large numbers of bitcoins to be created.[73] The artificially created bitcoins were removed when another chain overtook the bad chain.[74]

Based on bitcoin's open source code, other cryptocurrencies started to emerge in 2011.[23]

In March 2013, a technical glitch caused a fork in the block chain, with one half of the network adding blocks to one version of the chain and the other half adding to another. For six hours two bitcoin networks operated at the same time, each with its own version of the transaction history. The core developers called for a temporary halt to transactions, sparking a sharp sell-off. Normal operation was restored when the majority of the network downgraded to version 0.7 of the bitcoin software.[75]

In 2013 some mainstream websites began accepting bitcoins. WordPress had started in November 2012,[76] followed byOKCupid in April 2013,[77] Atomic Mall in November 2013,[78] TigerDirect[79] and Overstock.com in January 2014,[80] Expedia in June 2014,[81] Newegg and Dell in July 2014,[82] and Microsoft in December 2014.[83][note 13] Certain non-profit or advocacygroups such as the Electronic Frontier Foundation accept bitcoin donations.[85] (The organization started accepting bitcoins in January 2011,[86] stopped accepting them in June 2011,[87] and began again in May 2013.[85])

In May 2013, the Department of Homeland Security seized assets belonging to the Mt. Gox exchange.[88] The U.S. Federal Bureau of Investigation (FBI) shut down the Silk Road website in October 2013.[89]

In October 2013, Chinese internet giant Baidu had allowed clients of website security services to pay with bitcoins.[90] During November 2013, the China-based bitcoin exchange BTC China overtook the Japan-based Mt. Gox and the Europe-basedBitstamp to become the largest bitcoin trading exchange by trade volume.[91] On 19 November 2013, the value of a bitcoin on the Mt. Gox exchange soared to a peak of US$900 after a United States Senate committee hearing was told by the FBI that virtual currencies are a legitimate financial service.[92] On the same day, one bitcoin traded for over RMB¥6780 (US$1,100) in China.[93] On 5 December 2013, the People's Bank of China prohibited Chinese financial institutions from using bitcoins.[94] After the announcement, the value of bitcoins dropped,[95] and Baidu no longer accepted bitcoins for certain services.[96] Buying real-world goods with any virtual currency has been illegal in China since at least 2009.[97]

The first bitcoin ATM was installed in October 2013 in Vancouver, British Columbia, Canada.[98]

As of 2013 mining had become quite competitive and was compared to an arms race as ever-more-specialized technology was being utilized. The most efficient mining hardware makes use of custom designed application-specific integrated circuits, which outperform general purpose CPUs and also use less power.[99] Without access to these purpose-built machines, a bitcoin miner is unlikely to earn enough to even cover the cost of the electricity used in his or her efforts.[48]

With about 12 million existing bitcoins in November 2013,[100] the new price increased the market cap for bitcoin to at least US$7.2 billion.[101] By 23 November 2013, the total market capitalization of bitcoin exceeded US$10 billion for the first time.[102]

In the US two men were arrested in January 2014 on charges of money-laundering using bitcoins; one was Charlie Shrem, the head of now defunct bitcoin exchange BitInstant and a vice chairman of the Bitcoin Foundation. Shrem allegedly allowed the other arrested party to purchase large quantities of bitcoins for use on black-market websites.[103]

In early February 2014, one of the largest bitcoin exchanges, Mt. Gox,[104] suspended withdrawals citing technical issues.[105] By the end of the month, Mt. Gox had filed for bankruptcy protection in Japan amid reports that 744,000 bitcoins had been stolen.[106] Originally a site for trading **Magic: The Gathering** cards,[107] Mt. Gox had once been the dominant bitcoin exchange but its popularity had waned as users experienced difficulties withdrawing funds.[108]

On June 18, 2014, it was announced that bitcoin **payment service provider BitPay** would become the new sponsor of **St. Petersburg Bowl** under a two-year deal, renamed the Bitcoin St. Petersburg Bowl. Bitcoin was to be accepted for ticket and concession sales at the game as part of the sponsorship, and the sponsorship itself was also paid for using bitcoin.[109]

Less than one year after the collapse of Mt. Gox, **Bitstamp** announced that the exchange would be taken offline while they investigate a hack which resulted in about 19,000 bitcoins (equivalent to roughly US$5 million at that time) being stolen from their hot wallet.[110] The exchange remained offline for several days amid speculation that customers had lost their funds. Bitstamp resumed trading on January 9 after increasing security measures and ensuring customers that their account balances would not be impacted.[111]

The bitcoin exchange service **Coinbase** launched the first regulated bitcoin exchange in 25 US states on January 26th, 2015. At the time of the announcement, CEO Brian Armstrong stated that Coinbase intends to expand to thirty countries by the end of 2015.[112] A spokesperson for **Benjamin M. Lawsky**, the superintendent of the state's Department of Financial Services, stated that Coinbase is operating without a license in the state of New York. Lawsky is responsible for the development of the so-called 'BitLicense', which companies need to acquire in order to legally operate in New York.[113]

Economics

Classification

According to the director of the Institute for Money, Technology and Financial Inclusion at the University of California-Irvine there is "an unsettled debate about whether bitcoin is a currency".[114] Bitcoin is commonly referred to with terms like: digital currency,[14]:1 digital cash,[115] virtual currency,[4] electronic currency,[16] or cryptocurrency.[114] Its inventor, Satoshi Nakamoto, used the term electronic cash.[12] Bitcoins have 3 useful qualities in a currency, according to the Economist in 1/2015: they are "hard to earn, limited in supply and easy to verify".[116]

Economists define money as a store of value, a medium of exchange, and a unit of account and agree that bitcoin has some way to go to meet all these criteria.[117] It does best as a medium of exchange.[note 14] The bitcoin market currently suffers from volatility, limiting the ability of bitcoin to act as a stable store of value, and retailers accepting bitcoin use other currencies as their principal unit of account.[117]

Journalists and academics also dispute what to call bitcoin. Some media outlets do make a distinction between "real" money and bitcoins,[121] while other call bitcoin real money.[122] The Wall Street Journal declared it a commodity in December 2013.[123]A Forbes journalist referred to it as digital collectible.[124] Two University of Amsterdam computer scientists proposed the term "money-like informational commodity".[125]

The People's Bank of China has stated that bitcoin "is fundamentally not a currency but an investment target".[126]

Buying and selling

Bitcoins can be bought and sold both on- and offline. Participants in online **exchanges** offer bitcoin **buy and sell bids**. Using an online exchange to obtain bitcoins entails some risk, and, according to a study published in April 2013, 45% of exchanges fail and take client bitcoins with them.[127] Exchanges have since implemented measures to provide proof of reserves in an effort to convey transparency to users.[128] Offline, bitcoins may be purchased directly from an individual[129] or at a **bitcoin ATM**.[130]

Price and volatility

Price[note 15] and volatility[note 16]chart.[note 10] Left vertical axis: price, the scale is **logarithmic**. Right vertical axis: volatility. Horizontal axis: date ranging from 2010-08-17 to 2014-12-31.

To improve access to price information and increase transparency, on 30 April 2014Bloomberg LP announced plans to list prices from bitcoin companies Kraken andCoinbase on its 320,000 subscription financial data terminals.[131]

According to **Mark T. Williams**, as of 2014, bitcoin has **volatility** seven times greater than gold, eight times greater than the S&P 500, and eighteen times greater than the U.S. dollar.[132]

Attempting to explain the high volatility, a group of Japanese scholars stated that there is no stabilization mechanism.[133] The Bitcoin Foundation contends that high volatility is due to insufficient liquidity,[134] while a Forbes journalist claims that it is related to the uncertainty of its long-term value,[135] and the high volatility of a startup currency makes sense, "because people are still experimenting with the currency to figure out how useful it is."[136]

There are uses where volatility does not matter, such as online gambling, tipping, and international remittances.[136] As of 2014, pro-bitcoin venture capitalists argued that the greatly increased trading volume that planned high-frequency trading exchanges were hoped to bring would decrease price volatility.[131]

The price of bitcoins has gone through various cycles of appreciation and depreciation referred to by some as bubbles and busts.[137][138] In 2011, the value of one bitcoin rapidly rose from about US$0.30 to US$32 before returning to US$2.[139] In the latter half of 2012 and during the 2012-2013 Cypriot Financial Crisis, the bitcoin price began to rise,[140] reaching a high of US$266 on 10 April 2013, before crashing to around US$50.[141] On November 29, 2013, the cost of one bitcoin rose to the all-time peak of US$1,242.[142] In 2014 the price fell sharply, and as of April remained depressed at little more than half 2013 prices. As of August 2014 it was under US$600.[143] In January 2015, noting that the bitcoin price had dropped to its lowest level since spring 2013 - around US$224 - the New York Times suggested that "[w]ith no signs of a rally in the offing, the industry is bracing for the effects of a prolonged decline in prices. In particular, bitcoin mining companies, which are essential to the currency's underlying technology, are flashing warning signs."[144] Also in January 2015, Business Insider reported that deep web drug dealers were "freaking out" as they lost profits through being unable to convert bitcoin revenue to cash quickly enough as the price declined - and that there was a danger that dealers selling reserves to stay in business might force the bitcoin price down further.[145]

Speculative bubble dispute

Bitcoin has been labelled a *speculative bubble* by many including former Fed Chairman Alan Greenspan[146] and economistJohn Quiggin.[147] Nobel Laureate Robert Shiller said that bitcoin "exhibited many of the characteristics of a speculative bubble".[148] Two lead software developers of bitcoin, Gavin Andresen[149] and Mike Hearn,[150] have warned that bubbles may occur. David Andolfatto, a Vice President at the Federal Reserve Bank of St. Louis, stated, "Is bitcoin a bubble? Yes, if bubble is defined as a liquidity premium." According to Andolfatto, the price of bitcoin "consists purely of a bubble," but he concedes that many assets have prices that are greater than their intrinsic value.[39]:21 Journalist Matthew Boesler rejects the speculative bubble label and sees bitcoin's quick rise in price as nothing more than normal economic forces at work.[151] The Washington Post pointed out that the observed cycles of appreciation and depreciation don't correspond to the definition of speculative bubble.[139]

Ponzi scheme dispute

Various journalists,[152] U.S. economist Nouriel Roubini,[153] and the head of the Estonian central bank[154] have voiced concerns that bitcoin may be a Ponzi scheme. A 2012 report by the European Central Bank had stated, "it [is not] easy to assess whether or not the bitcoin system actually works like a pyramid or Ponzi scheme."[155]:27 A 2014 report by the World Bank concluded that "contrary to a widely-held opinion, bitcoin is not a deliberate Ponzi".[156]:7 In the opinion of Eric Posner, a law professor at the University of Chicago "A real Ponzi scheme takes fraud; bitcoin, by contrast, seems more like a collective delusion."[152]

U.S. economist Nouriel Roubini, former senior adviser to the U.S. Treasury and the International Monetary Fund, has stated that bitcoin is "a Ponzi game".[157] In February 2014 an asset-manager and columnist for The New York Post called bitcoin a Ponzi scheme opining, "Welcome to 21st-century Ponzi scheme: Bitcoin".[158] The head of the Estonian central bank, Mihkel Nommela, stated, "virtual currency schemes are an innovation that deserves some caution, given the lack of ... evidence that this isn't just a Ponzi scheme."[154]

Others have expressed the opinion that bitcoin is not a Ponzi scheme. The Huffington Post asked, "is bitcoin a Ponzi scheme, yes or no?" answering the question with a definitive "no!".[159] PC World magazine stated, "bitcoin is clearly not a Ponzi scheme".[160] Economist Jeffrey Tucker claims that "there are several key differences between a Ponzi scheme and bitcoin."[161] A 2014 report by Federal Council (Switzerland) states, "the question is repeatedly raised whether bitcoin can be deemed an impermissible pyramid scheme... since in the case of bitcoin the typical promises of profits are lacking, it cannot be assumed that bitcoin is a pyramid scheme."[162]:21

Value forecasts

Financial journalists and analysts, economists, and investors have attempted to predict the possible future value of bitcoin. In April 2013, economist John Quiggin stated, "bitcoins will attain their true value of zero sooner or later, but it is impossible to say when".[147] A similar forecast was made in November 2014 by economist Kevin Dowd.[163] In

November 2014, David Yermack, Professor of finance at NYU Stern School of Business forecast that in November 2015 bitcoin may be all but worthless.[164] In December 2013, finance professor Mark T. Williams forecast a bitcoin would be worth less than ten U.S. dollars by July 2014.[165] In the indicated period bitcoin has exchanged as low as $344 (April 2014) and during July 2014 the bitcoin low has been $609.[note 10][166] In December 2014 professor Williams said: "The probability of success is low, but if it does hit, the reward will be very large."[167] In May 2013, Bank of America FX and Rate Strategist David Woo forecast a maximum fair value per bitcoin of $1,300.[168] Bitcoin investor Cameron Winklevoss stated in December 2013 that the "[s]mall bull case scenario for bitcoin is... 40,000 USD a coin".[169]

Obituaries

The "death" of bitcoin has been proclaimed numerous times.[170] Forbes declared bitcoin dead in June 2011,[171] followed by Gizmodo Australia in August 2011.[172] Wired wrote it had expired in December 2012,[173] Ouishare Magazine declared, "game over, bitcoin" in May 2013,[174] and New York Magazine stated bitcoin was on its path to grave in June 2013.[175] Reuters published an "obituary" for bitcoin in January 2014[176] Street Insider declared bitcoin dead in February 2014,[177] as did the Weekly Standard in March 2014,[178] followed by Salon in March 2014,[179] and Vice News in March 2014,[180] then the Financial Times in September 2014, and 9 others.[181] In January 2015, USA Today termed bitcoin "to be headed to the ash heap",[182]and The Telegraph declared it was "the end of bitcoin experiment".[183] One journalist has recorded 29 such "obituaries" as of early 2015.[170]

Reception

Some economists have responded positively to bitcoin, but many have not. François R. Velde, Senior Economist at the Chicago Fed described it as "an elegant solution to the problem of creating a digital currency".[184] According to Wired "in the estimation of many leading economists, bitcoin is a fatally flawed idea shaped by people who don't really understand how money works".[185] Paul Krugman and Brad DeLong have found fault with bitcoin questioning why it should act as a reasonably stable store of value or whether there is a floor on its value.[186] Economist John Quiggin has criticized bitcoin as "the final refutation of the efficient-market hypothesis".[147]

David Andolfatto, Vice President at the Federal Reserve Bank of St. Louis, stated that bitcoin is a threat to the establishment, which he argues is a good thing for the Federal Reserve System and other central banks because it prompts these institutions to operate sound policies.[39]:33[187][188]

Free software movement activist Richard Stallman has criticized the lack of anonymity and called for reformed development.[189] PayPal President David A. Marcus calls bitcoin a "great place to put assets" but claims it will not be a currency until price volatility is reduced.[190] Bill Gates, in relation to the cost of moving money from place to place in an interview for Bloomberg L.P. stated: "Bitcoin is exciting because it shows how cheap it can be."[191]

Similarly, **Peter Schiff**, a bitcoin sceptic understands "the value of the technology as a payment platform" and his Euro Pacific Precious Metals fund partnered with **BitPay** in May 2014, because "a wire transfer of fiat funds can be slow and expensive for the customer".[192]

Kevin Dowd, Professor of Finance and economics at Durham University has a bearish outlook on bitcoin as a currency. At the **Cato Institute**'s 2014 Annual Conference with the topic 'Alternatives to Central Banking: Toward Free-Market Money'[193] he said "bitcoin's current incentive structure [is] leading to an inevitable collapse, mostly due to the centralization of mining".[194]

A bitcoin ATM in Vienna – Westbahnhof

Acceptance by merchants

Alexa rank ⬍	Site ⬍
33[98]	PayPal[99]
41[100]	Microsoft[101]
328[102]	Dell[103]
329[104]	Newegg[105]
505[106]	Overstock.com[107]
512[108]	Expedia[109]
1,981[110]	TigerDirect[111]
5,674[112]	Dish Network[113]
7,038[114]	Zynga[115]
30,565[116]	Time Inc.[117]
176,903[118]	PrivateFly[119]
253,983[120]	Virgin Galactic[121]
348,010[122]	Dynamite Entertainment[123]
1,145,668[124]	Clearly Canadian[125]
n.a.	Sacramento Kings[126]

Bitcoins are accepted in this **café** in the **Netherlands** as of 2013

In 2015, the number of merchants accepting bitcoin exceeded 100,000.[195] As of December

Due to the fact that **chargebacks** are impossible, retailers usually offer in-store cr: as the only option when returning items purchased with bitcoins.[207]

As of September 2014 **PayPal** allows North American merchants using its system the ability to receive payment in bitcoins.[208]

Organizations accepting donations in bitcoin include: **Greenpeace**,[209] The **Mozilla Foundation**,[210] and **The Wikimedia Foundation**.[211] Some U.S. political candidates, including New York City Democratic Congressional candidate **Jeff Kurzon** have said they would accept campaign donations in bitcoin.[212] In late 2013 the **University of Nicosia** became the first university in the world to accept bitcoins.[213]

Mainstream use of bitcoin

Fewer than 5,000 bitcoins per day (worth roughly $1.2 million on 18 February 2015) are being used for retail transactions, according to estimates by Tim Swanson, head of business development at Melotic, a Hong Kong-based cryptocurrency technology company. After a fourfold growth in 2013, retail volume in 2014 has seen only a little, if any, increase.[214]

Financial institutions

Bitcoin companies have had difficulty opening traditional bank accounts because lenders have been leery of bitcoin's links to illicit activity.[215] According to Antonio Gallippi, a co-founder of BitPay, "banks are scared to deal with bitcoin companies, even if they really want to".[216] In 2014, the National Australia Bank closed accounts of businesses with ties to bitcoin, and HSBCrefused to serve a hedge fund with links to bitcoin.[217]

One financial institution has been bullish on bitcoin. In a 2013 report, Bank of America Merrill Lynch stated that "we believe bitcoin can become a major means of payment for e-commerce and may emerge as a serious competitor to traditional money-transfer providers."[218] In June 2014, the first bank that converts deposits in currencies instantly to bitcoin without any fees was opened in Boston.[219]

As investment

Some Argentinians have bought bitcoins to protect their savings against high inflation or the possibility that governments could confiscate savings accounts.[63] During the 2012–2013 Cypriot financial crisis, bitcoin purchases in Cyprus rose due to fears that savings accounts would be confiscated or taxed.[220] Other methods of investment are bitcoin funds. The first regulated bitcoin fund was established in Jersey in July 2014 and approved by the Jersey Financial Services Commission.[221] Also, c. 2012 an attempt was made by the Winklevoss twins (who in April 2013 claimed they owned nearly 1% of all bitcoins in existence[222]) to establish a bitcoin ETF.[223] As of early 2015, they have announced plans to launch a New York based bitcoin exchange named Gemini. [224]

In 2013 and 2014, the European Banking Authority[28] and the Financial Industry Regulatory Authority (FINRA), a United States self-regulatory organization,[225] warned that investing in bitcoins carries significant risks. Such risks were highlighted in 2014 when Bloomberg named bitcoin as one of its worst investments of the year,[226] although Forbes named bitcoin the best investment of 2013.[227] Bloomberg selected the Russian ruble as the worst currency investment of 2014 but also mentioned bitcoin as the "one currency that did worse [than the ruble] in 2014, depending on whether you think virtual currencies are real money."[226]

Venture capital

Venture capitalists, such as Peter Thiel's Founders Fund, which invested US$3 million in BitPay, do not purchase bitcoins themselves, instead funding bitcoin infrastructure like companies that provide payment systems to merchants, exchanges, wallet services, etc.[228] In 2012, an incubator for bitcoin-focused start-ups was founded by Adam Draper, with financing help from his father, venture capitalist Tim Draper, one of the largest bitcoin holders after winning an auction of 30,000 bitcoins,[229]at the time called 'mystery buyer'.[230] The company's goal is to fund 100 bitcoin businesses within 2–3 years with $10,000 to $20,000 for a 6% stake.[229] Investors also invest in bitcoin mining.[231]

Political economy

Bitcoin appeals to tech-savvy libertarians, because it so far exists outside the institutional banking system and the control of governments.[232] However, researchers looking to uncover the reasons for interest in bitcoin did not find evidence that this was linked to libertarianism.[233]

Bitcoin's appeal reaches from **left wing critics**, "who perceive the state and banking sector as representing the same elite interests, [...] recognising in it the potential for collective **direct democratic** governance of currency"[234] and socialists proposing their "own states, complete with currencies",[235] to right wing critics suspicious of **big government**, at a time when activities within the regulated banking system were responsible for the severity of the **financial crisis of 2007–08**,[236] "because governments are not fully living up to the responsibility that comes with state-sponsored money".[237] Bitcoin has been described as "remov[ing] the imbalance between the big boys of finance and the disenfranchised little man, potentially allowing early adopters to negotiate favourable rates on exchanges and transfers – something that only the very biggest firms have traditionally enjoyed".[238] Two WSJ journalists describe bitcoin in their book as "about freeing people from the tyranny of centralised trust".[239]

Legal status and regulation

Main article: Legality of bitcoin by country

Various government agencies, departments, and courts have treated bitcoin differently. A few governments have moved to regulate bitcoin and similar payment systems. According to the **European Central Bank**, traditional financial sector regulation is not applicable because bitcoin does not involve traditional financial actors.[155]:5 Others in the EU have stated, however, that existing rules can be extended to include bitcoin and bitcoin companies.[240]

Steven Strauss, a Harvard public policy professor, suggested in April, 2013, that governments could outlaw bitcoin,[241] and this possibility was mentioned again in a July, 2013, report to a regulator made by a prospective bitcoin investment vehicle.[223]However, the vast majority of nations have not done so as of 2014. It is illegal in at least seven countries:

Bangladesh,[242]Bolivia,[243] Ecuador,[244] Iceland,[245] Kyrgyzstan,[246] Russia ,[245] and Vietnam.[247]

Australia[:]

Australia classifies bitcoin as property and an asset for capital gains purposes, however capital gains or losses arising from personal use of bitcoins is disregarded providing the cost of the bitcoins was less than $10,000.[248]

China[:]

While private parties can hold and trade bitcoins in China, regulation prohibits financial firms like banks from doing the same.[245] On 5 December 2013, China Central Bank made its first step in regulating bitcoin by prohibiting financial institutions from handling bitcoin transactions.[249] In a statement on the central bank's website the People's Bank of China said financial institutions and payment companies cannot give pricing in, buy and sell bitcoin or insure bitcoin-linked products. A December 2013 statement from BTC China suggested payment processors had voluntarily withdrawn their services.[250] On 1 April 2014 China Central Bank ordered commercial banks and payment companies to close bitcoin trading accounts in two weeks.[251]Trading bitcoins by individuals is legal in China.[249]

European Union[:]

The European Central Bank classifies bitcoin as a convertible decentralized virtual currency.[155]:6 A German court found bitcoin to be a unit of account.[34]:10 The Finnish government judged it to be a commodity not a currency.[252] In July 2014 theEuropean Banking Authority advised European banks not to deal in virtual currencies such as bitcoin until a regulatory regime was in place.[253]

G7[:]

In 2013 the G7's Financial Action Task Force issued the following statement in guidelines which may be applicable to companies involved in transmitting bitcoin and other currencies, "Internet-based payment services that allow third party funding from anonymous sources may face an increased risk of [money laundering/terrorist financing]." They concluded that this may "pose challenges to countries in [anti-money laundering/counter terrorist financing] regulation and supervision".[254]

Iceland[:]

As of 2014, foreign exchange activities with bitcoin is illegal in Iceland.[245]

Russia[:]

As of 2014, bitcoin is illegal in this country.[245]

Taiwan[:]

While bitcoin itself is not illegal here, approvals for bitcoin ATMs have been refused.[245]

United States[:]

The U.S. Treasury classifies bitcoin as a convertible decentralized virtual currency.[1] Magistrate Judge Amos L. Mazzant of a Texas District Court classified bitcoin as a currency.[255] A June 2014 U.S. government auction of almost 30,000 bitcoins, which the U.S. Marshals Service seized in October 2013 from Silk Road, was said to increase legitimacy of the currency.[230]

The U.S. Government Accountability Office (GAO) reviewed virtual currencies upon the request of the Senate Finance Committee and in May 2013 recommended, that the Internal Revenue Service (IRS) formulate tax guidance for bitcoin businesses.[256] On 25 March 2014, in time for 2013 tax filing, the IRS issued a guidance that virtual currency is treated as property for U.S. federal tax purposes and that "an individual who 'mines' virtual currency as a trade or business [is] subject to self-employment tax".[257]

On 18 November 2013, the United States Senate held a committee hearing titled "Beyond Silk Road: Potential Risks, Threats and Promises of Virtual Currencies" to discuss virtual currencies.[258] At this hearing, held by senator Tom Carper, bitcoin and other currencies were received generally positively, with statements that bitcoin was a "legal means of exchange" and that "online payment systems, both centralized and decentralized, offer legitimate financial services" by US officials Peter Kadzik andMythili Raman.[100][259]

The **Federal Election Commission** (FEC) deadlocked on 21 November 2013 on whether to allow bitcoin in political campaigns. Their decision was split across party lines (three members Democrat voting nay, three Republicans voting yea).[260] Political bitcoin pioneers New Hampshire House member Mark Warden[261] and Southern California politician Michael B. Glenn[262]independently from each other accepted bitcoin in their campaigns, and paved the way for others to follow suit. On 8 May 2014, the U.S. Federal Election Commission issued draft guidance to U.S. politicians who want to receive bitcoin donations.[263] The Commission declined to declare bitcoins currency, stating they fit into its "anything of value" definition.[264]

In May 2014, Brett Stapper, co-founder of Falcon Global Capital, registered to lobby members of Congress and federal agencies on issues related to bitcoin.[265]

In January 2014, the U.S. **Securities and Exchange Commission** (SEC) was focused on whether bitcoin-denominated stock exchanges were illegal, per its enforcement administrator, and inquired into unregistered securities offerings of the gambling site SatoshiDICE and FeedZeBirds.[266] In May it warned investors that "both fraudsters and promoters of high-risk investment schemes may target bitcoin users".[267] The SEC charged and settled with the former owner of SatoshiDice and FeedZeBirds in June 2014 for selling unregistered securities.[268] In October 2014, former SEC Chair **Arthur Levitt** joined **BitPay**, a bitcoin payment processor, and Vaurum, a bitcoin exchange for institutional investors in advisory roles.[269]

The U.S. **Commodity Futures Trading Commission** stated in March 2014 it considered regulation of digital currencies[270] after TeraExchange announced to launch a **swap**. TeraExchange constructed an index for the value of bitcoin from six different exchanges. The dollar value of a given bitcoin amount is locked in the swap. The CFTC approved the financial product in September 2014, satisfied it "could not easily be manipulated".[271]

In June 2014 California Assemblyman **Roger Dickinson** (D–Sacramento) submitted draft legislation **(Assembly Bill 129)** to legalize bitcoin and all other forms of alternative and digital currency.[272] After the GAO had called for increased oversight of bitcoin, the **Consumer Financial Protection Bureau** warned consumers of bitcoin being risky.[273]

As of November 2014, there are no final rules at the U.S. state level yet. In March 2014, the **New York State Department of Financial Services** led by superintendent **Benjamin Lawsky** had officially invited bitcoin exchanges to apply with them,[274] and on 17 July it published draft regulations for virtual currency businesses.[275] Businesses would have to provide transaction receipts, disclosures about risks, policies to handle customer complaints, maintain a cybersecurity program, hire a compliance officer and verify details about their customers to follow anti-money-laundering rules, per FinCEN.[275]

Vietnam[:]

As of 2014, bitcoin is illegal in this country.[245]

Criminal activity[:]

The use of bitcoin by criminals has attracted the attention of financial regulators, legislative bodies, law enforcement, and the media.[29] The FBI prepared an intelligence assessment,[31] the SEC has issued a pointed warning about investment schemes using virtual currencies,[29] the U.S. Senate held a hearing on virtual currencies in November 2013, **CNN** has referred to bitcoin as a "shady online currency [that is] starting to gain legitimacy in certain parts of the world",[276] and **The Washington Post** called it "the currency of choice for seedy online activities".[32] Criminal activity involving bitcoin has centered around theft and the use of bitcoins in exchange for illegal items or services.[citation needed]

Several news outlets have asserted that the popularity of bitcoins hinges on the ability to use them to purchase illegal goods.[277][278] In 2014 researchers at the University of Kentucky found "robust evidence that computer programming enthusiasts and illegal activity drive interest in bitcoin, and find limited or no support for political and investment motives."[233]

Theft[:]

There have been many cases of bitcoin theft.[56] One way this is accomplished involves a third party accessing the private key to a victim's bitcoin address,[279] or of an online wallet.[280] If the private key is stolen, all the bitcoins from the compromised address can be transferred. In that case, the network does not have any provisions to identify the thief, block further transactions of those stolen bitcoins, or return them to the legitimate owner.[223]

Theft also occurs at sites bitcoins are used to purchase illicit goods. In late November 2013, an estimated $100 million in bitcoins were stolen from the online illicit goods marketplace **Sheep Marketplace**, which immediately closed.[281] Users tracked the coins as they were processed and converted to cash, but no funds were recovered and no culprits identified.[281] A different black market, Silk Road 2, stated that during a February 2014 hack, bitcoins valued at $2.7 million were taken from escrow accounts.[282] Inputs.io, an Australian bitcoin wallet service was hacked twice in October 2013 and lost more than $1 million in bitcoins.[283]

Sites where users exchange bitcoins for cash are another target for theft. In late February 2014 Mt. Gox, one of the largest virtual currency exchanges, filed for bankruptcy in Tokyo amid reports that 744,000 bitcoins had been stolen.[106] Flexcoin, a bitcoin storage specialist based in Alberta, Canada, shut down on March 2014 after saying it discovered a theft of about $650,000 in bitcoins.[284] Poloniex, a digital currency exchange, reported on March 2014 that it lost bitcoins valued at around $50,000.[285] In January, 2015, UK based bitstamp, the third busiest bitcoin exchange globally, was hacked and 19,000 bitcoins ($5 million) were stolen.[286] February, 2015, saw a Chinese exchange named BTER lose more than 7,000 bitcoins to hackers.[287]

Black markets[:]

Because of its presumed capacity to obfuscate the source of payments in online transactions, bitcoin has come to be used in the deep web black markets.[citation needed] It was estimated that in 2012, 4.5% to 9% of all transactions on all exchanges in the world were for drug trades on a single deep web drugs market, Silk Road.[288] Child pornography, murder-for-hire services, and weapons are also available on black market sites that sell in bitcoin.[289]

Several deep web black markets have been shut by authorities. In October 2013 Silk Road was shut down by U.S. law enforcement[290][291][292] leading to a short-term decrease in the value of bitcoin.[293] Alternative sites were soon available, and in early 2014 the **Australian Broadcasting Corporation** reported that the closure of Silk Road had little impact on the number of Australians selling drugs online, which had actually increased.[294] In early 2014, Dutch authorities closed Utopia, an online illegal goods market, and seized 900 bitcoins.[295] In late 2014, a joint police operation saw European and American authorities seize bitcoins and close 400 **deep web** sites including the illicit goods market Silk Road 2.0.[296] Law enforcement activity has resulted in several convictions. In December, 2014, **Charlie Shrem** was sentenced to two years in prison for indirectly helping to send $1 million to the Silk Road drugs site,[297] and in February, 2015, its founder, **Ross Ulbricht**, was convicted on drugs charges and faces a life sentence.[298]

Some black market sites may seek to steal bitcoins from customers. The bitcoin community branded one site, Sheep Marketplace, as a scam when it prevented withdrawals and shut down after an alleged bitcoins theft.[299] In a separate case, escrow accounts with bitcoins belonging to patrons of a different black market were hacked in early 2014.[282]

According to the **Internet Watch Foundation**, a U.K. based charity, bitcoin is used to purchase child pornography, and almost 200 such websites accept it as payment. Bitcoin isn't the sole way to purchase child pornography online, as Troels Oertling, head of the cybercrime unit at **Europol**, states, "Ukash and Paysafecard... have [also] been used to pay for such material." However, the Internet Watch Foundation lists around 30 sites that exclusively accept bitcoins.[300] Some of these sites have shut down, such as a **deep web crowdfunding** website that aimed to fund the creation of new child porn.[301] Furthermore, **hyperlinks** to child porn websites have been added to the blockchain as arbitrary data can be included when a transaction is made.[302][303]

Money laundering[:]

Bitcoins may not be ideal for money laundering because all transactions are public.[304] Authorities, including the European Banking Authority[28] and the FBI[31] have expressed concerns that bitcoin may be used for money laundering. In early 2014, an operator of a U.S. bitcoin exchange was arrested for money laundering.[103]

Ponzi scheme[:]

In a Ponzi scheme that utilized bitcoins, The Bitcoin Savings and Trust promised investors up to 7 percent weekly interest, and raised at least 700,000 bitcoins from 2011 to 2012.[305] In July 2013 the U.S. Securities and Exchange Commission charged the company and its founder in 2013 "with defrauding investors in a Ponzi scheme involving bitcoin".[305] In September 2014 the judge fined Bitcoin Savings & Trust and its owner $40 million for operating a bitcoin Ponzi scheme.[306]

Malware[:]

Bitcoin-related malware includes software that steals bitcoins from users using a variety of techniques, software that uses infected computers to mine bitcoins, and different types of ransomware, which disable computers or prevent files from being accessed until some payment is made. Security company Dell SecureWorks said in February 2014 that it had identified almost 150 types of bitcoin malware.[307]

Unauthorized mining[:]

In June 2011, **Symantec** warned about the possibility that **botnets** could mine covertly for bitcoins.[308] Malware used the **parallel processing** capabilities of GPUs built into many modern **video cards**.[309] Although the average PC with an integrated graphics processor is virtually useless for bitcoin mining, tens of thousands of PCs laden with mining malware could produce some results.[310]

In mid-August 2011, bitcoin mining botnets were detected,[311] and less than three months later, bitcoin mining **trojans** had infected Mac OS X.[312]

In April 2013, **electronic sports** organization E-Sports Entertainment was accused of hijacking 14,000 computers to mine bitcoins; the company later settled the case with the State of New Jersey.[313]

German police arrested two people in December 2013 who customized existing botnet software to perform bitcoin mining, which police said had been used to mine at least $950,000 worth of bitcoins.[314]

For four days in December 2013 and January 2014, Yahoo! Europe hosted an ad containing bitcoin mining malware that infected an estimated two million computers.[310] The software, called **Sefnit**, was first detected in mid-2013 and has been bundled with many software packages. Microsoft has been removing the malware through its **Microsoft Security Essentials** and other security software.[315]

Several reports of employees or students using university or research computers to mine bitcoins have been published.[316]

Malware stealing[:]

Some malware can steal private keys for bitcoin wallets allowing the bitcoins themselves to be stolen. The most common type searches computers for cryptocurrency wallets to upload to a remote server where they can be cracked and their coins stolen.[317] Many of these also **log keystrokes** to record passwords, often avoiding the need to crack the keys.[317] A different approach detects when a bitcoin address is copied to a **clipboard** and quickly replaces it with a different address, tricking people into sending bitcoins to the wrong address.[318] This method is effective because bitcoin transactions are irreversible.

One **virus**, spread through the Pony **botnet**, was reported in February 2014 to have stolen up to $220,000 in cryptocurrencies including bitcoins from 85 wallets.[319] Security company **Trustwave**, which tracked the malware, reports that its latest version was able to steal 30 types of digital currency.[320]

A type of Mac malware active in August 2013, Bitvanity posed as a vanity wallet address generator and stole addresses and private keys from other bitcoin client software.[321] A different trojan for Mac OS X, called CoinThief was reported in February 2014 to be responsible for multiple bitcoin thefts.[321] The software was hidden in versions of some cryptocurrency apps onDownload.com and MacUpdate.[321]

Ransomware[:]

Another type of bitcoin-related malware is **ransomware**. One program called **CryptoLocker**, typically spread through legitimate-looking email attachments, encrypts the hard drive of an infected computer, then displays a countdown timer and demands a ransom, usually two bitcoins, to decrypt it.[322] Massachusetts police said they paid a 2 bitcoin ransom in November 2013, worth more than $1,300 at the time, to decrypt one of their hard drives.[323] Linkup, a combination ransomware and bitcoin mining program that surfaced in February 2014, disables internet access and demands cr: card information to restore it, while secretly mining bitcoins.[322]

Security[:]

Various potential attacks on the **bitcoin network** and its use as a payment system, real or theoretical, have been considered. The bitcoin protocol includes several features that protect it against some of those attacks, such as unauthorized spending, double spending, forging bitcoins, and tampering with the block chain.[41] Other attacks, such as theft of private keys, require due care by users.

Unauthorized spending[:]

Unauthorized spending is mitigated by bitcoin's implementation of public-private key cryptography. When Alice sends a bitcoin to Bob, Bob becomes the new owner of the bitcoin. Eve observing the transaction might want to spend the bitcoin Bob just received, but she cannot sign the transaction without the knowledge of Bob's private key.[14]

Double spending[:]

A specific problem that an internet payment system must solve is **double-spending**, whereby a user pays the same coin to two or more different recipients. An example of such a problem would be if Eve sent a bitcoin to Alice and later sent the same bitcoin to Bob. The bitcoin network guards against double-spending by recording all bitcoin transfers in a ledger (the block chain) that is visible to all users, and ensuring for all transferred bitcoins that they haven't been previously spent.[14]:4

Race attack[:]

If Eve offers to pay Alice a bitcoin in exchange for goods and signs a corresponding transaction, it is still possible that she also creates a different transaction at the same time sending the same bitcoin to Bob. By the rules, the network accepts only one of the transactions. This is called race attack, since there is a race which transaction will be accepted first. Alice can reduce the risk of race attack stipulating that she will not deliver the goods until Eve's payment to Alice appears in the block chain.[324]

A variant race attack (which has been called a Finney attack by reference to Hal Finney) requires the participation of a miner. Instead of sending both payment requests (to pay Bob and Alice with the same coins) to the network, Eve issues only Alice's payment request to the network, while the accomplice tries to mine a block that includes the payment to Bob instead of Alice. There is a positive probability that the rogue miner will succeed before the network, in which case the payment to Alice will be rejected. As with the plain double-spending attack, Alice can reduce the risk of a Finney attack by waiting for the payment to be included in the block chain.[325]

History modification[:]

The other principal way to steal bitcoins would be to modify block chain ledger entries.

For example, Eve could buy something from Alice, like a sofa, by adding a signed entry to the block chain ledger equivalent to *Eve pays Alice 100 bitcoins*. Later, after receiving the sofa, Eve could modify that block chain ledger entry to read instead: *Eve pays Alice 1 bitcoin*, or replace Alice's address by another of Eve's addresses. Digital signatures cannot prevent this attack: Eve can simply sign her entry again after modifying it.

To prevent modification attacks, each block of transactions that is added to the block chain includes a **cryptographic hash code** that is computed from the hash of the previous block as well as all the information in the block itself. When the bitcoin software notices two competing block chains, it will automatically assume that the chain with the greatest amount of work to produce it is the valid one. Therefore, in order to modify an already recorded transaction (as in the above example), the attacker would have to recalculate not just the modified block, but all the blocks after the modified one, until the modified chain contains more work than the legitimate chain that the rest of the network has been building in the meantime. Consequently, for this attack to succeed, the attacker must outperform the honest part of the network.[41]

Each block that is added to the block chain, starting with the block containing a given transaction, is called a confirmation of that transaction. Ideally, merchants and services that receive payment in bitcoin should wait for at least one confirmation to be distributed over the network, before assuming that the payment was done. The more confirmations that the merchant waits for, the more difficult it is for an attacker to successfully reverse the transaction in a block chain—unless the attacker controls more than half the total network power, in which case it is called a 51% attack.[326] For example, if the attacker possesses 10% of the calculation power of the bitcoin network and the shop requires 6 confirmations for a successful transaction, the probability of success of such an attack will be 0.02428%.[12]

Selfish mining[:]

This attack was first introduced by Ittay Eyal and Emin Gun Sirer at the beginning of November 2013.[327] The attacker does not normally broadcast the blocks upon finding them. He mines his private chain and eventually (when somebody finds his own block) publishes several blocks at row. This makes the "honest" network abandon their last work and switch to the attacker's branch. As a result, honest miners lose a significant part of their revenue, whilst the attacker increases profits due to changes in relative hashpowers.

According to the authors it changes the incentives for rational miners and makes them want to join the attacker's pool, increasing attacker's hashpower (which could potentially lead to **51% attack**).

However, other researchers disagree with the conclusion and point out the flaws in the article.[328]

Deanonymisation of clients[:]

Along with transaction graph analysis, which may reveal connections between bitcoin addresses (pseudonyms),[2][329] there is a possible attack[330] which links user pseudonym to its **IP address**, even if the peer is using **Tor**. The attack makes use of bitcoin mechanisms of relaying peer addresses and anti-**DoS** protection. The cost of the attack on the full bitcoin network is under €1500 per month.[330]

In the media[:]

A bitcoin documentary film called The Rise and Rise of Bitcoin made its debut at the Tribeca Film Festival in New York on 23 April 2014, chronicling its origins to its explosive growth in 2013.[331]

Several lighthearted songs celebrating bitcoin have been released.[332] Numerous U.S. comedians have made fun of "bitcoin confusion".[333]

In Fall 2014, undergraduate students at the Massachusetts Institute of Technology (MIT) each received bitcoins worth $100 "to better understand this emerging technology". One student had the idea of a Bitcoin Club and raised more than half a million dollars from an MIT alumnus working in high-frequency trading.[334]

In Season 3 CBS show The Good Wife featured an episode alluding to the creator of bitcoin as well as the FBI investigating the case. The episode titled 'Bitcoin for Dummies' was telecasted on January 15, 2012.[335]

On February 19th, 2015, Morgan Spurlock aired an episode about bitcoin on his CNN docu-series, Inside Man. Filmed in July 2014, the episode features Morgan living off of nothing but bitcoin for a week to figure out whether the world is ready for a new kind of money.

The Future – 1 BTC = $100,000 and MilliBitcoin?

- Bitcoin could hit $100,000 in 10 years, says the analyst who correctly called its $2,000 price

- Bitcoin could make up 10 percent of the $5 trillion average daily volume in the foreign exchange market in 10 years, according to Saxo Bank analyst Kay Van-Petersen.

- Its market capitalization could grow to $1.75 trillion which would make each bitcoin worth

- Bitcoin's price has the potential to hit over $100,000 in 10 years, which would mark a 3,483 percent rise from its recent record high, an analyst who correctly predicted the cryptocurrency's rally this year told CNBC on Tuesday.

- In December, Saxo Bank published its annual report called "Outrageous Predictions" with one of the forecasts calling for bitcoin to hit $2,000 in 2017. At the time the note was published, bitcoin was trading at around $754, so the target price represented a 165 percent rise. Bitcoin hit $2,000 on May 20.

- But now, Kay Van-Petersen, the analyst behind the call, is looking long term and sees a big rise ahead for bitcoin.

- How will bitcoin hit $100,000

- Here's how he came up with his price target in 10 years.

- Van-Petersen is assuming cryptocurrencies in general – not just bitcoin – will account for 10 percent of the average daily volumes (ADV) of fiat currency trade in 10 years. Foreign exchange ADV currently stands at just over $5 trillion, according to the Bank for International Settlements.

- Ten percent of $5 trillion is $500 billion. This is the ADV that cryptocurrencies could have. Bitcoin will account for 35 percent of that market share, which would that $175 billion of the $500 billion figure, he said. This would mean that $175 billion worth of bitcoin would be traded every day

- Also, Van-Petersen then implies that bitcoin's market capitalization would be ten times the average daily volume, giving a figure of $1.75 trillion for the market cap. The current figure is around $37.8 billion, according to data from industry website CoinDesk.

- Bitcoin has a limited supply of 21 million which is expected to be reached by the year 2140. In 10 years, the analyst thinks that there will be 17 million bitcoin in circulation, up from the current 16.3 million figure.

- If the potential 17 million of bitcoins in supply is divided by the $1.75 trillion market cap

- Van-Petersen – who owns bitcoin – emphasizes that this is a rough calculation but that his growth predictions could be "conservative" given that in the year 2013 alone, bitcoin's price grew over 5,000 percent. The analyst said that cryptocurrencies will survive in the long run.

- "This is not a fad, cryptocurrencies are here to stay," Van-Petersen told CNBC in a phone interview.

- "There will emerge two to three main ones. Bitcoin will be one of those. And the reason is the first-mover advantage, the scale and the pioneering."

-

- Bitcoin surges 11% to all-time high above $2,700; Has now doubled in May   Thursday, 25 May 2017 | 11:20 AM ET | 00:35

- Van-Petersen's views are not the official view of Saxo Bank, the analyst said.

- Bitcoin's bad reputation

- The bitcoin industry has had its fair share of problems and reputational damage. The digital currency has often had an image of being used for illegal means such as buying drugs online. The collapse of Mt.Gox in 2014, once the world's largest bitcoin exchange, is still fresh in the minds of users. Some members of the exchange are still waiting for compensation.

- More recent issues include some exchanges not allowing people to withdraw their money in fiat currency. On top of this, the view of bitcoin as a currency for criminals is still prevalent after the major WannaCry ransomware cyberattack saw hackers lock peoples' files and ask for bitcoin in exchange to unlock them.

- Still, Van-Petersen says that the industry is still extremely young and big improvements will come. A few factors will boost bitcoin adoption including better wallets, easier methods to buy the digital currency, use of it for money transfers in areas like remittances, as well as citizens of countries with volatile economies and currencies buying it.

- "Volumes are going up, volatility is going down. A lot of people talk about the volatility, but if you are in Zimbabwe or Venezuela, this volatility is nothing. This is the interesting thing to me. I think in the West, a lot of people view it is as speculative, but emerging markets will get it, their needs will be different," Van-Petersen added.

- While Van-Petersen is offering one way to value bitcoin in the future, others say that there are other factors to take into consideration.

- "It's one way of slicing the pie to try and predict future prices which always relies on a lot of assumptions," Charlie Hayter, CEO of industry website CryptoCompare, told CNBC by email.

- "Equating volumes to price value is one method of attempting a valuation, but it doesn't take into account the fundamentals of the ecosystem."

- The fundamentals of what bitcoin is capable of from a technical point of view and how regulation is molded around its use will determine its value too, Hayter added.

MilliBitcoins

- Buying and selling using whole bitcoins as the preferred unit of currency might have made sense back when a single bitcoin was valued at just $10 to $20 USD.

- These days, though, when bitcoins trade for well over $100 apiece, a smaller unit could prove more user-friendly for commerce, many Bitcoiners say.

- While we're probably not yet ready for the satoshi -- 1/100,000,000th of a bitcoin -- conducting transactions in mBTC, or 1/1,000th of a bitcoin, seems easier somehow.

- For example, how would you rather see a cup of coffee priced at the "Bitcoin Cafe" ... as 0.01 BTC, or as 10 mBTC?

- For many of us, it just seems to make more sense psychologically to transact in 10 of something than in 1/100ths of something.

- That's why some people in the Bitcoin community are advocating a change to the mBTC as the unit of choice in their economy.

- Jeff Coleman - AKA eMansipater - has lead the movement.

- Posting on reddit's Bitcoin subreddit, user DanielTaylor wrote June 2 (Sunday) as "mBTC day" ... a "proposed voluntary day to change to mBTC in speech, websites and applications." Many others immediately embraced the idea.

- "Moving to mBTC is one of the most important non-technical changes that Bitcoin could make in my opinion," wrote redditor aminok.

- The idea has also won support from more than half of those responding to a Bitcoin Forum poll suggesting the mBTC as the standard denomination. In response to the question, "Should we start using mBTC as the standard denomination?", 53.1 percent said "Yes" as of the morning of June 2. Another 19.9 percent chose "After the price is at $1,000, dollar parity for the mBTC," 7.4 percent said "After the price is somewhat higher, $250+" and 7.1 percent responded, "In a few months if the price grows or remains stable."

- Another 11.4 percent split their answers among, "No. Maybe much later." "No. Never." and "I'm not sure." And 1.2 percent supported an option added to the poll later: "Switch to XBT." (An XBT is 100 satoshi, or 1,000,000th of a bitcoin.)

- Bitcoin Forum member Razick, who posted the poll, said in an email to CoinDesk that support for a switch to the mBTC "seems to be across the board in general," though he noted the poll itself did not request additional elaboration from respondents.

- "Overall it is very positive with the vast majority supporting a change in the somewhat near future either to mBTC or XBT (ISO compliant designation for uBTC)," Razick said. "At this time, my poll indicates that over 60% support a switch either immediately or over the next few months."

- Of those who prefer to keep the bitcoin as the main unit of currency for now, Razick added, "I believe the primary motive is to avoid confusion or affect the exchange rate. Some individuals prefer an organic change driven by Bitcoin users naturally beginning to use mBTC without encouragement from retailers and software developers."

- Like many others posting on the forum, reddit and elsewhere, Razick see a shift to mBTC as a way to help promote Bitcoin's adoption by more users.

- "The goal of changing in the near term is to make prices and exchange rates more attractive to newcomers in order to help accelerate growth," he said. "Bitcoin's high exchange rate is a psychological barrier to market entry that is holding Bitcoin adoption back. It is also somewhat inconvenient to deal with prices such as 0.01435 BTC when making a purchase; wouldn't 14.35 mBTC be more attractive? Lastly, laymen have a hard time understanding Bitcoin's 21 million unit limit. They think of it as a barrier to widespread Bitcoin use since it's not immediately obvious just how divisible Bitcoin is. Using mBTC it immediately becomes clear that there are at least 21 billion units. Problem solved."

The other Cryptocurrencies in the Market

#	Name	Market Cap	Price as off May 29, 2017
1	Bitcoin	$37,196,444,973	$2273.71

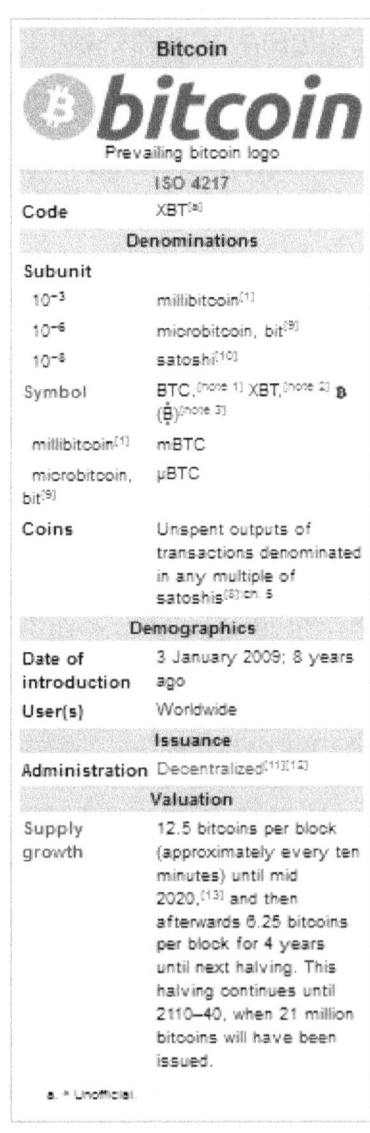

◆ Ethereum

Ethereum

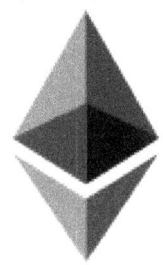

The Ethereum Project's logo, first used in 2014.

Initial release	30 July 2015
Repository	github.com/ethereum /go-ethereum🔗
Development status	Active
Written in	C++, Go, Rust
Operating system	Clients available for Linux, Windows, macOS, POSIX, Raspbian
Platform	x86, ARM
Type	Decentralized computing
License	Multiple open-source licenses
Website	www.ethereum.org🔗

2

Ethereum is an open-source, public, blockchain-based distributed computing platform featuring smart contract (scripting) functionality.[1] It provides a decentralized Turing-complete virtual machine, the Ethereum Virtual Machine (EVM), which can execute scripts using an international network of public nodes. Ethereum also provides a cryptocurrency token called "ether", which can be transferred between accounts and used to compensate participant nodes for computations performed. Gas, an internal transaction pricing mechanism, is used to prevent spam and allocate resources on the network.[1][2]

Ethereum was proposed in late 2013 by Vitalik Buterin, a cryptocurrency researcher and programmer. Development was funded by an online crowdsale during July–August 2014.[3] The system went live on 30 July 2015.

In 2016 Ethereum was forked into two blockchains, as a result of the collapse of The DAO project. The two chains have different numbers of users, and the minority fork was renamed to Ethereum Classic[4]. The majority fork has retained the name Ethereum (the subject of this article).[5][6][7][8]

Ether:

The value token of the Ethereum blockchain is called ether. It is listed under the diminutive ETH and traded on **cryptocurrency** exchanges. It is also used to pay for transaction fees and computational services on the Ethereum network.[9]

Tokens can be volatile per circumstances, such as ether's plunge from $21.50 to $8 when **The DAO** was hacked on June 17, 2016

Ripple

Original author(s)	Arthur Britto, David Schwartz, Ryan Fugger
Developer(s)	Ripple
Initial release	2012
Stable release	0.60.0[1] / 2017[1]
Repository	github.com/ripple /rippled🔗
Development status	Active
Operating system	Server: GNU/Linux (RHEL, CentOS, Ubuntu), OS X (development only)
Type	Real-time gross settlement, currency exchange, remittance
License	ISC license[2]
Website	Ripple.com🔗

Ripple is a real-time gross settlement system (RTGS), currency exchange and remittance network operated by Ripple. Also called the **Ripple Transaction Protocol (RTXP)** or **Ripple protocol**,[3] it is built upon a distributed open source Internet protocol, consensus ledger and native currency called **XRP** (ripples). Released in 2012, Ripple purports to enable "secure, instant and nearly free global financial transactions of any size with no chargebacks." It supports tokens representing fiat currency, cryptocurrency, commodity or any other unit of value such as frequent flier miles or mobile minutes.[4][5] At its core, Ripple is based around a shared, public database or ledger,[6] which uses a consensus process that allows for payments, exchanges and remittance in a distributed process.[7]

In 2014, Ripple defended the security of its consensus algorithm against rival Stellar Networks.[8][9] Currently, Ripple's XRP tokens are the third-largest currency by market capitalization,[10][11] after bitcoin and ethereum.[12][13][14]

Used by companies such as UniCr:, UBS or Santander, the Ripple protocol has been increasingly adopted by banks and payment networks as settlement infrastructure technology, [16] with *American Banker* explaining that "from banks' perspective, distributed ledgers like the Ripple system have a number of advantages over cryptocurrencies like bitcoin," including price and security.[17]

In February 2015, Fidor Bank announced they would be using the Ripple protocol to implement a new real-time international money transfer network,[47] and in late April 2015, it was announced that Western Union was planning to "experiment" with Ripple.[37] In late May 2015, Commonwealth Bank of Australia announced it would be experimenting with Ripple[48] in relation to intrabank transfers.[49] Since 2012, representatives of Ripple Labs have professed support for government regulation of the crypto-currency market, claiming that regulations help businesses grow.[50] On May 5, 2015, FinCEN fined Ripple Labs and XRP II US$700,000 for violation of the Bank Secrecy Act,[31] based on the Financial Crimes Enforcement Network's additions to the act in 2013.[51] Ripple Labs agreed to remedial steps to ensure future compliance, which included an agreement to only transact XRP and "Ripple Trade" activity through registered money services businesses (MSB), among other agreements such as enhancing the Ripple Protocol.[31] The enhancement won't change the protocol itself, but will instead add AML transaction monitoring to the network and improve transaction analysis.[51] As of 2017, the current release of the server (known as rippled) is version 0.40.0.[1]

The year 2015 and 2016 marked the expansion of Ripple (company) with the opening of an office in Sydney, Australia in April 2015[52] and the opening of European offices in London, United Kingdom in March 2016[53] then in Luxembourg in June 2016.[54] Many companies have subsequently announced experimenting and integrations with Ripple.[55]

 NEM $1,891,539,000 $0.210171

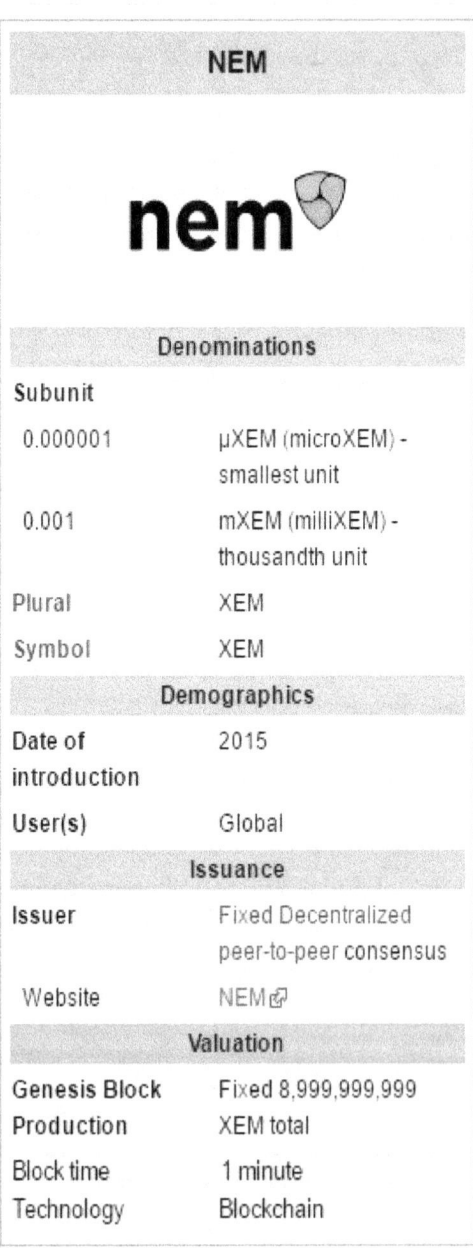

NEM	
Denominations	
Subunit	
0.000001	µXEM (microXEM) - smallest unit
0.001	mXEM (milliXEM) - thousandth unit
Plural	XEM
Symbol	XEM
Demographics	
Date of introduction	2015
User(s)	Global
Issuance	
Issuer	Fixed Decentralized peer-to-peer consensus
Website	NEM⤤
Valuation	
Genesis Block Production	Fixed 8,999,999,999 XEM total
Block time	1 minute
Technology	Blockchain

NEM is a peer-to
peer cryptocurrency and blockchain platform launched on
March 31, 2015.[1] Written in Java,[2] with a C++ version in
the works,[3] NEM has a stated goal of a wide distribution
model and has introduced new features
to blockchain technology such as its proof-of-importance
(POI) algorithm, multisignature accounts, encrypted
messaging, and an Eigentrust++ reputation system. The
NEM blockchain software is used in a commercial
blockchain called Mijin,[4] which is being tested by financial
institutions and private companies in Japan and
internationally.[5]

Architecture:

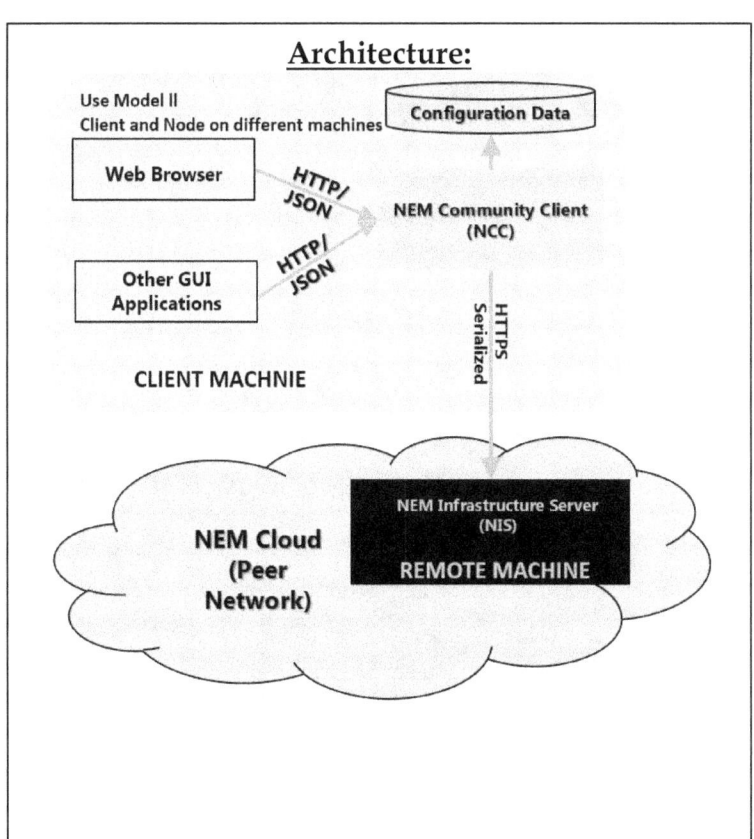

Ethereum Classic $1,555,400,563 $16.89

Ethereum Classic

The Ethereum Classic logo

Initial release	30 July 2015
Development status	Active
Written in	C++, Go, Rust
Operating system	Clients available for Linux, Windows, macOS, POSIX, Raspbian
Platform	x86, ARM
Type	Decentralized computing
License	Multiple open-source licenses
Website	ethereumclassic .github.io

Ethereum Classic (ETC) is an open-source, public, blockchain-based distributed computing platform featuring smart contract (scripting) functionality.[1][2] It provides a decentralized Turing-complete virtual machine, the Ethereum Virtual Machine (EVM), which can execute scripts using an international network of public nodes. Ethereum Classic also provides a value token called "classic ether", which can be transferred between participants and is used to compensate participant nodes for computations performed. Gas, an internal transaction pricing mechanism, is used to prevent spam on the network and allocate resources proportionally to the incentive offered by the request.[3][4][5][6] It is the 6th largest cryptocurrency by market cap.[7][8]

Ethereum Classic came into existence as a result of the DAO hard-fork.[9][10] It consolidated members of the Ethereum community who rejected the DAO Hard Fork on philosophical grounds. The reasons of which were stated in the Ethereum Classic Declaration of Independence.[11] People who held Ether from before the DAO hard fork have both a balance of Ethereum Classic (ETC) in addition to an equal amount of Ethereum (ETH) . Exchanges that held customer funds in Ethereum also held in their control a proportional quantity of ETC after the hard fork but may have lost significant amounts due to the lack of replay protection that was not programmed in the DAO Hard Fork code released by the Ethereum Foundation and exchanges lack of knowledge of how to separate ETC from ETH and secure it.[12] Users at most ETH exchanges have demanded their ETC be made available to them.[13] As of 1 February 2017, both Ethers are actively traded.[14]

6	Litecoin	$1,279,667,253	$24.93
7	Dash	$857,516,426	$117.06
8	Monero	$616,684,254	$42.41
9	Bytecoin	$446,839,010	$0.002442
10	Golem	$385,880,071	$0.467806
11	Stellar Lumens	$364,597,567	$0.037729
12	Stratis	$362,941,786	$3.69
13	Dogecoin	$296,115,228	$0.002702
14	Zcash	$285,598,779	$202.68
15	Waves	$271,894,000	$2.72

16	Gnosis	$244,275,660	$221.15
17	Augur	$233,493,700	$21.23
18	Steem	$228,978,700	$0.977741
19	Siacoin	$212,944,576	$0.008060
20	GameCr:s	$174,529,653	$2.77
21	MaidSafeCoin	$171,452,197	$0.378856
22	BitShares	$170,799,082	$0.065640
23	DigixDAO	$150,666,400	$75.33
24	DigiByte	$126,834,514	$0.015645
25	Lisk	$116,049,454	$1.08
26	Factom	$113,566,014	$12.97

27	BitConnect	$110,950,382	$17.28
28	Ardor	$108,186,650	$0.108295
29	Tether	$108,086,804	$1.03
30	Decred	$105,148,493	$21.04
31	Iconomi	$102,661,740	$1.18
32	SingularDTV	$99,493,800	$0.165823
33	PIVX	$95,590,843	$1.79
34	Round	$93,366,550	$0.109843
35	Byteball	$65,220,596	$344.56
36	Nxt	$62,002,235	$0.062064
37	Aragon	$61,065,965	$1.82

38	SysCoin	$59,551,729	$0.113413
39	FirstBlood	$55,711,590	$0.651153
40	Komodo	$49,622,390	$0.491576
41	AntShares	$47,422,400	$0.948448
42	iExec RLC	$38,429,801	$0.492243
43	Peercoin	$37,809,263	$1.57
44	ReddCoin	$35,296,863	$0.001238
45	Emercoin	$34,084,278	$0.849199
46	Melon	$33,943,123	$56.63
47	Lykke	$33,495,226	$0.243004
	BitcoinDark	$30,289,421	$23.50

49	Storjcoin X	$28,844,254	$0.563660
50	Xaurum	$25,358,360	$0.223020
51	Wings	$25,353,279	$0.282619
52	Namecoin	$24,692,901	$1.68
53	Counterparty	$24,125,378	$9.21
54	TokenCard	$23,706,713	$1.00
55	Gulden	$23,663,073	$0.068323
56	Nexus	$22,301,361	$0.448157
57	Ark	$22,184,355	$0.232950
58	Ubiq	$21,586,432	$0.582340
59	WeTrust	$20,639,105	$0.223979

Edgeless	$19,608,631	$0.249345
EarthCoin	$19,580,664	$0.002095
Synereo	$19,443,585	$0.236378
YbCoin	$19,182,605	$6.35
Unity Ingot	$19,011,594	$0.094117
BCAP	$18,908,500	$1.89
Humaniq	$18,597,910	$0.152784
BitBay	$18,027,590	$0.017893
Matchpool	$17,232,375	$0.229765
Infinitecoin	$17,180,496	$0.000190
Burst	$17,155,003	$0.009649

71	PotCoin	$16,965,210	$0.078210
72	Swarm City	$16,740,730	$2.53
73	NAV Coin	$16,602,653	$0.271197
74	Pepe Cash	$15,809,657	$0.022525
75	Blocknet	$15,287,812	$3.91
76	GridCoin	$14,994,957	$0.038418
77	BlackCoin	$14,868,749	$0.195226
78	Agoras Tokens	$14,452,578	$0.344109
79	Expanse	$13,951,537	$1.93
80	I/O Coin	$13,864,028	$0.848708

81	◇ LBRY Cr:s	$13,383,456	$0.195309
82	◎ Chronobank	$13,269,949	$18.69
83	ⓏZCoin	$13,191,076	$5.97
84	⬡ Bitland	$13,058,400	$0.435280
85	❀ Etheroll	$13,044,933	$1.86
86	◯ MonaCoin	$12,970,295	$0.257482
87	◎ E-coin	$12,946,056	$4.73
88	◉ Bankcoin	$12,919,439	$3.03
89	● E-Dinar Coin	$12,590,380	$0.027421
90	✇ Verge	$12,305,256	$0.000918
91	◈ Nexium	$11,495,662	$0.172811

92	Vertcoin	$11,473,581	$0.343122
93	TaaS	$11,459,387	$1.41
94	FedoraCoin	$10,813,614	$0.000024
95	Pluton	$10,725,294	$12.62
96	Energycoin	$10,150,288	$0.083934
97	Radium	$10,100,399	$3.11
98	MergeCoin	$10,082,347	$0.102306
99	vSlice	$10,031,473	$0.300429
100	Omni	$10,026,410	$17.94

References **Bitcoin**

1.   ^ ********** to:ᵃ ᵇ *Siluk, Shirley (2 June 2013). "June 2 "M Day" promotes millibitcoin as unit of choice". CoinDesk. Retrieved 25 May 2017.*

2.   **********^ *Nermin Hajdarbegovic (7 October 2014). "Bitcoin Foundation to Standardise Bitcoin Symbol and Code Next Year". CoinDesk. Retrieved 28 January 2015.*

3.   **********^ *Romain Dillet (9 August 2013). "Bitcoin Ticker Available On Bloomberg Terminal For Employees". TechCrunch. Retrieved 2 November 2014.*

4.   **********^ *"Bitcoin Composite Quote (XBT)". CNN Money. CNN. Retrieved 2 November 2014.*

5.   **********^ *"XBT – Bitcoin". xe.com. Retrieved 2 November 2014.*

6.   **********^ *Shirriff, Ken (2 October 2015). "Proposal for addition of bitcoin sign"* (PDF). *unicode.org.* Unicode. *Retrieved 3 November 2015.*

7.   **********^ *"Proposed New Characters: Pipeline Table". unicode.org. Unicode Inc. Retrieved 30 November 2016.*

8.   ^ ********** to:ᵃ ᵇ ᶜ ᵈ ᵉ ᶠ ᵍ ʰ ⁱ ʲ *Andreas M. Antonopoulos (April 2014). Mastering Bitcoin. Unlocking Digital Crypto-Currencies. O'Reilly Media.* ISBN 978-1-4493-7404-4.

9.   **********^ *Garzik, Jeff (2 May 2014). "BitPay, Bitcoin, and where to put that decimal point". Retrieved 20 November 2015.*

10.   ^ ********** to:ᵃ ᵇ ᶜ *Jason Mick (12 June 2011). "Cracking the Bitcoin: Digging Into a $131M USD Virtual Currency". Daily Tech. Retrieved 30 September 2012.*

11.   ^ ********** to:ᵃ ᵇ *"Statement of Jennifer Shasky Calvery, Director Financial Crimes Enforcement Network United States Department of the Treasury Before the United States Senate Committee on Banking, Housing, and Urban Affairs Subcommittee on National Security and International Trade and Finance Subcommittee on Economic Policy"* (PDF). *fincen.gov. Financial Crimes Enforcement Network. 19 November 2013. Retrieved 1 June 2014.*

12. **********^ Empson, Rip (28 March 2013). "Bitcoin: How An Unregulated, Decentralized Virtual Currency Just Became A Billion Dollar Market". TechCrunch. AOL inc. Retrieved 8 October 2016.

13. **********^ Ron Dorit; Adi Shamir (2012). "Quantitative Analysis of the Full Bitcoin Transaction Graph" (PDF). Cryptology ePrint Archive. Retrieved 18 October 2012.

14. ^ ********** to:[a b c d e f g] Jerry Brito & Andrea Castillo (2013). "Bitcoin: A Primer for Policymakers" (PDF). Mercatus Center. George Mason University. Retrieved 22 October 2013.

15. ^ ********** to:[a b c] S., L. (2 November 2015). "Who is Satoshi Nakamoto?". The Economist. The Economist Newspaper Limited. Retrieved 23 September 2016.

16. ^ ********** to:[a b c d e] Davis, Joshua (10 October 2011). "The Crypto-Currency: Bitcoin and its mysterious inventor". The New Yorker. Retrieved 31 October 2014.

17. ^ ********** to:[a b] Sagona-Stophel, Katherine. "Bitcoin 101 white paper" (PDF). Thomson Reuters. Retrieved 20 November 2015.

18. **********^ "What is Bitcoin?". CNN Money. Retrieved 16 November 2015.

19. **********^ Natasha Lomas (16 September 2013). "BitPay Passes 10,000 Bitcoin-Accepting Merchants On Its Payment Processing Network". Techcrunch. Techcrunch.com. Retrieved 21 October 2013.

20. ^ ********** to:[a b c] Lee, Timothy B. (21 November 2013). "Here's how Bitcoin charmed Washington". The Washington Post. Retrieved 10 October 2016.

21. ^ ********** to:[a b c] Cuthbertson, Anthony (4 February 2015). "Bitcoin now accepted by 100,000 merchants worldwide". International Business Times. IBTimes Co., Ltd. Retrieved 20 November 2015.

22. ^ ********** to:[a b] Hileman, Garrick; Rauchs, Michel. "Global Cryptocurrency Benchmarking Study" (PDF). Cambridge University. Retrieved 14 April 2017.

23. ^ ********** to:[a b] "bitcoin". OxfordDictionaries.com. Retrieved 28 December 2014.

24. ^ ********** to:[a b c d e] Nakamoto, Satoshi (October 2008). "Bitcoin: A Peer-to-Peer Electronic Cash System" (PDF). bitcoin.org. Retrieved 28 April 2014.

25. ^ ********** to:ᵃ ᵇ Bustillos, Maria (2 April 2013). *"The Bitcoin Boom"*. *The New Yorker*. Condé Nast. Retrieved 22 December 2013. *Standards vary, but there seems to be a consensus forming around Bitcoin, capitalized, for the system, the software, and the network it runs on, and bitcoin, lowercase, for the currency itself.*

26. **********^ Vigna, Paul (3 March 2014). *"BitBeat: Is It Bitcoin, or bitcoin? The Orthography of the Cryptography"*. *WSJ*. Retrieved 21 April 2014.

27. **********^ Metcalf, Allan (14 April 2014). *"The latest style"*. Lingua Franca blog. *The Chronicle of Higher Education* (chronicle.com). Retrieved 19 April 2014.

28. ^ ********** to:ᵃ ᵇ ᶜ ᵈ ᵉ ᶠ *"The great chain of being sure about things"*. *The Economist*. The Economist Newspaper Limited. 31 October 2015. Retrieved 3 July 2016.

29. **********^ *"Bitcoin Wallet"*. *Investopedia*. Retrieved 28 June 2016.

30. **********^ Sparkes, Matthew (9 June 2014). *"The coming digital anarchy"*. *The Telegraph*. London: Telegraph Media Group Limited. Retrieved 7 January 2015.

31. ^ ********** to:ᵃ ᵇ ᶜ ᵈ ᵉ *"Charts"*. *Blockchain.info*. Retrieved 2 November 2014.

32. ^ ********** to:ᵃ ᵇ ᶜ ᵈ ᵉ Joshua A. Kroll; Ian C. Davey; Edward W. Felten (11–12 June 2013). *"The Economics of Bitcoin Mining, or Bitcoin in the Presence of Adversaries"* (PDF). The Twelfth Workshop on the Economics of Information Security (WEIS 2013). Retrieved 26 April 2016. *A transaction fee is like a tip or gratuity left for the miner.*

33. **********^ *"Regulation of Bitcoin in Selected Jurisdictions"* (PDF). The Law Library of Congress, Global Legal Research Center. January 2014. Retrieved 26 August 2014.

34. **********^ Katie Pisa & Natasha Maguder (9 July 2014). *"Bitcoin your way to a double espresso"*. cnn.com. CNN. Retrieved 23 April 2015.

35. **********^ Andolfatto, David (31 March 2014). *"Bitcoin and Beyond: The Possibilities and Pitfalls of Virtual Currencies"* (PDF). Dialogue with the Fed. Federal Reserve Bank of St. Louis. Retrieved 16 April 2014.

36. **********^ *"Difficulty History"* (The ratio of all hashes over valid hashes is D x 4295032833, where D is the published "Difficulty" figure.). *Blockchain.info. Retrieved 26 March 2015.*

37. **********^ Hampton, Nikolai (5 September 2016). *"Understanding the blockchain hype: Why much of it is nothing more than snake oil and spin". Computerworld. IDG. Retrieved 5 September 2016.*

38. **********^ Ashlee Vance (14 November 2013). *"2014 Outlook: Bitcoin Mining Chips, a High-Tech Arms Race". Businessweek. Retrieved 24 November 2013.*

39. **********^ *"Block #420000". Blockchain.info. Retrieved 11 September 2016.*

40. **********^ Ritchie S. King; Sam Williams; David Yanofsky (17 December 2013). *"By reading this article, you're mining bitcoins". qz.com. Atlantic Media Co. Retrieved 17 December 2013.*

41. **********^ Shin, Laura (24 May 2016). *"Bitcoin Production Will Drop By Half In July, How Will That Affect The Price?". Forbes. Retrieved 13 July 2016.*

42. **********^ Adam Serwer & Dana Liebelson (10 April 2013). *"Bitcoin, Explained". motherjones.com. Mother Jones. Retrieved 26 April 2014.*

43. ^ ********** to:[a] [b] [c] Villasenor, John (26 April 2014). *"Secure Bitcoin Storage: A Q&A With Three Bitcoin Company CEOs". forbes.com. Forbes. Retrieved 26 April 2014.*

44. **********^ *"Bitcoin: Bitcoin under pressure". The Economist. 30 November 2013. Retrieved 30 November 2013.*

45. ^ ********** to:[a] [b] [c] Skudnov, Rostislav (2012). *Bitcoin Clients* (PDF) *(Bachelor's Thesis). Turku University of Applied Sciences. Retrieved 16 January 2014.*

46. **********^ *"Blockchain Size". Blockchain.info. Retrieved 24 April 2016.*

47. **********^ *"Wallet Pruning in v0.12.0". bitcoin.org. Retrieved 8 January 2017.*

48. **********^ Gervais, Arthur; O. Karame, Ghassan; Gruber, Damian; Capkun, Srdjan. *"On the Privacy Provisions of Bloom Filters in Lightweight Bitcoin Clients"* (PDF). *Retrieved 3 September 2016.*

49. **********^ *Jon Matonis (26 April 2012). "Be Your Own Bank: Bitcoin Wallet for Apple". Forbes. Retrieved 17 November 2014.*

50. **********^ *Bill Barhydt (4 June 2014). "3 reasons Wall Street can't stay away from bitcoin". NBCUniversal. Retrieved 2 April 2015.*

51. **********^ *"MtGox gives bankruptcy details". bbc.com. BBC. 4 March 2014. Retrieved 13 March 2014.*

52. **********^ *Staff, Verge (13 December 2013). "Casascius, maker of shiny physical bitcoins, shut down by Treasury Department". The Verge. Retrieved 10 January 2014.*

53. **********^ *Eric Mu (15 October 2014). "Meet Trezor, A Bitcoin Safe That Fits Into Your Pocket". Forbes Asia. Forbes. Retrieved 31 October 2014.*

54. **********^ *"Bitcoin Core version 0.9.0 released". bitcoin.org. Retrieved 8 January 2015.*

55. **********^ *Metz, Cade (19 August 2015). "The Bitcoin Schism Shows the Genius of Open Source". Wired. Condé Nast. Retrieved 3 July 2016.*

56. **********^ *Vigna, Paul (17 January 2016). "Is Bitcoin Breaking Up?". The Wall Street Journal. Retrieved 8 November 2016.*

57. **********^ *Bajpai, Prableen (26 October 2016). "What Is Bitcoin Unlimited?". Investopedia, LLC. Retrieved 8 November 2016.*

58. **********^ *Allison, Ian (28 April 2017). "Ethereum co-founder Dr Gavin Wood and company release Parity Bitcoin". International Business Times. Retrieved 28 April 2017.*

59. **********^ *"Man Throws Away 7,500 Bitcoins, Now Worth $7.5 Million". CBS DC. 29 November 2013. Retrieved 23 January 2014.*

60. **********^ *O'Brien, Matt (13 June 2015). "The scam called Bitcoin". Daily Herald. Retrieved 20 September 2016.*

61. **********^ *Joshua Kopstein (12 December 2013). "The Mission to Decentralize the Internet". The New Yorker. Retrieved 30 December 2014. The network's 'nodes'—users running the bitcoin software on their computers—collectively check the integrity of other nodes to ensure that no one spends the same coins twice. All transactions are published on a shared public ledger, called the 'blockchain'.*

62.   **********^ *Gervais, Arthur; Karame, Ghassan O.; Capkun, Vedran; Capkun, Srdjan. "Is Bitcoin a Decentralized Currency?". InfoQ. InfoQ & IEEE computer society. Retrieved 11 October 2016.*

63.   **********^ *Simonite, Tom (5 September 2013). "Mapping the Bitcoin Economy Could Reveal Users' Identities". MIT Technology Review. Retrieved 2 April 2014.*

64.   ^ ********** to:ᵃ ᵇ *Lee, Timothy (21 August 2013). "Five surprising facts about Bitcoin". The Washington Post. Retrieved 2 April 2014.*

65.   **********^ *McMillan, Robert (6 June 2013). "How Bitcoin lets you spy on careless companies". wired.co.uk. Conde Nast. Retrieved 2 April 2014.*

66.   **********^ *Potts, Jake (31 July 2015). "Mastering Bitcoin Privacy". Airbitz. Retrieved 23 February 2016.*

67.   **********^ *Matonis, Jon (5 June 2013). "The Politics Of Bitcoin Mixing Services". forbes.com. Forbes. Retrieved 2 April 2014.*

68.   **********^ *Gaby G. Dagher, Benedikt Bünz, Joseph Bonneau, Jeremy Clark and Dan Boneh (26 October 2015). "Provisions: Privacy-preserving proofs of solvency for Bitcoin exchanges" (PDF). International Association for Cryptologic Research. Retrieved 23 February 2016.*

69.   **********^ *Blystone, Dan. "Bitcoin Transactions Vs. Cr: Card Transactions". Investopedia. Retrieved 3 September 2016.*

70.   **********^ *Ben-Sasson, Eli; Chiesa, Alessandro; Garman, Christina; Green, Matthew; Miers, Ian; Tromer, Eran; Virza, Madars (2014). "Zerocash: Decentralized Anonymous Payments from Bitcoin" (PDF). 2014 IEEE Symposium on Security and Privacy. IEEE computer society. Retrieved 31 October 2014.*

71.   **********^ *Miers, Ian; Garman, Christina; Green, Matthew; Rubin, Aviel. "Zerocoin: Anonymous Distributed E-Cash from Bitcoin" (PDF). Johns Hopkins University. Retrieved 15 February 2015.*

72.   **********^ *Greenberg, Andy (29 April 2014). "'Dark Wallet' Is About to Make Bitcoin Money Laundering Easier Than Ever". Wired. Retrieved 15 February 2015.*

73.   ^ ********** to:ᵃ ᵇ *Odell, Matt (21 September 2015). "A Solution To Bitcoin's Governance Problem". TechCrunch. Retrieved 24 January 2016.*

74.   **********^ *"Why the Bitcoin Block Size Debate Matters"*. Bitcoin Magazine. 7 July 2016. Retrieved 24 January 2016.

75.   ^ ********** to:[a] [b] Hayes, Adam (18 October 2016). *"The Three Major Bitcoin Protocols Explained"*. Investopedia. Retrieved 18 January 2017.

76.   **********^ Jordan Pearson (14 October 2016). *"'Bitcoin Unlimited' Hopes to Save Bitcoin from Itself"*. Motherboard. Vice Media LLC. Retrieved 17 January 2017.

77.   **********^ Vigna, Paul; Casey, Michael J. (January 2015). The Age of Cryptocurrency: How Bitcoin and Digital Money Are Challenging the Global Economic Order (1 ed.). New York: St. Martin's Press. **ISBN 978-1-250-06563-6**.

78.   ^ ********** to:[a] [b] Wallace, Benjamin (23 November 2011). *"The Rise and Fall of Bitcoin"*. Wired. **Archived** from the original on 2013-10-31. Retrieved 13 October 2012.

79.   **********^ *"Block 0 – Bitcoin Block Explorer"*. **Archived** from the original on 2013-10-15.

80.   **********^ Nakamoto, Satoshi (9 January 2009). *"Bitcoin v0.1 released"*. **Archived** from the original on 2014-03-26.

81.   **********^ *"SourceForge.net: Bitcoin"*. **Archived** from the original on 2013-03-16.

82.   **********^ Peterson, Andrea (3 January 2014). *"Hal Finney received the first Bitcoin transaction. Here's how he describes it."*. The Washington Post.

83.   **********^ Popper, Nathaniel (30 August 2014). *"Hal Finney, Cryptographer and Bitcoin Pioneer, Dies at 58"*. NYTimes. Retrieved 2 September 2014.

84.   **********^ Wallace, Benjamin (23 November 2011). *"The Rise and Fall of Bitcoin"*. Wired. Retrieved 4 November 2013.

85.   **********^ McMillan, Robert. *"Who Owns the World's Biggest Bitcoin Wallet? The FBI"*. Wired. Condé Nast. Retrieved 7 October 2016.

86.   **********^ Bosker, Bianca (16 April 2013). *"Gavin Andresen, Bitcoin Architect: Meet The Man Bringing You Bitcoin (And Getting Paid In It)"*. The Huffington Post. Retrieved 21 October 2016.

87.   ^ ********** to:*a b* Sawyer, Matt (26 February 2013). *"The Beginners Guide To Bitcoin – Everything You Need To Know"*. Monetarism. Archivedfrom the original on 2014-04-09.

88.   ^ ********** to:*a b* *"Vulnerability Summary for CVE-2010-5139"*. National Vulnerability Database. 8 June 2012. Archived from the original on 2014-04-09. Retrieved 22 March 2013.

89.   **********^ Nakamoto, Satoshi. *"ALERT — we are investigating a problem"*. Archived from the original on 2013-10-15. Retrieved 15 October 2013.

90.   **********^ Groom, Nelson (9 December 2015). *"Revealed, the elusive creator of Bitcoin: Founder of digital currency is named as an Australian academic after police raid his Sydney home"*. Daily Mail Australia. Retrieved 4 January 2016.

91.   ^ ********** to:*a b* *"Monetarists Anonymous"*. The Economist. The Economist Newspaper Limited. 29 September 2012. Retrieved 21 October 2013.

92.   **********^ Murphy, Kate (31 July 2013). *"Virtual Currency Gains Ground in Actual World"*. The New York Times. Retrieved 6 May 2014. A type of digital cash, bitcoins were invented in 2009 and can be sent directly to anyone, anywhere in the world.

93.   ^ ********** to:*a b* Joyner, April (25 April 2014). *"How bitcoin is moving money in Africa"*. usatoday.com. USA Today. Retrieved 25 May 2014.

94.   **********^ *"The magic of mining"*. The Economist. 13 January 2015. Retrieved 13 January 2015.

95.   ^ ********** to:*a b* *"Free Exchange. Money from nothing. Chronic deflation may keep Bitcoin from displacing its rivals."*. The Economist. 15 March 2014. Retrieved 25 March 2014.

96.   **********^ Wingfield, Nick (30 October 2013). *"Bitcoin Pursues the Mainstream"*. The New York Times. Retrieved 4 November 2013.

97.   **********^ Stephanie Lo & J. Christina Wang (September 2014). *"Bitcoin as Money?"* (PDF). Current Policy Perspectives (Federal Reserve Bank of Boston). **14** (1): 6.

98.   **********^ paypal at Alexa

99.   **********^ Scott Ellison (23 September 2014). *"PayPal and Virtual Currency"*. PayPal. Retrieved 31 October 2014.

100.	**********^ microsoft at Alexa

101.	**********^ Tom Warren (11 December 2014). "Microsoft now accepts Bitcoin to buy Xbox games and Windows apps". The Verge. Vox Media. Retrieved 11 December 2014.

102.	**********^ dell at Alexa

103.	**********^ Sydney Ember (18 July 2014). "Dell Begins Accepting Bitcoin". New York Times. Retrieved 18 July 2014.

104.	**********^ newegg at Alexa

105.	**********^ "Newegg accepts bitcoins". newegg.com. 1 July 2014. Retrieved 3 July 2014.

106.	**********^ overstock at Alexa

107.	**********^ Vaishampayan, Saumya (9 January 2014). "Bitcoin now accepted on Overstock.com through VC-backed Coinbase". marketwatch.com. Wall Street Journal. Retrieved 10 February 2014.

108.	**********^ expedia at Alexa

109.	**********^ Paul Vigna (11 June 2014). "Expedia Starts Accepting Bitcoin for Hotel Bookings". Money Beat. The Wall Street Journal. Retrieved 27 July 2014.

110.	**********^ tigerdirect at Alexa

111.	**********^ Jane McEntegart (26 January 2014). "TigerDirect is Now Accepting Bitcoin As Payment". Tom's hardware. Retrieved 28 August 2014.

112.	**********^ dish at Alexa

113.	**********^ Casey, Michael (29 May 2014). "Dish Network to Accept Bitcoin Payments". The Wall Street Journal. Dow Jones & Company. Retrieved 15 February 2015.

114.	**********^ zynga at Alexa

115.	**********^ Kharif, Olga (6 January 2014). "Bitcoin Tops $1,000 Again as Zynga Accepts Virtual Money". bloomberg.com. Bloomberg LP. Retrieved 20 January 2014.

116.	**********^ timeinc at Alexa

117.	**********^ Ember, Sydney (16 December 2014). "Time Inc. begins accepting bitcoin payments". Dealbook. The New York Times. Retrieved 9 January 2015.

118.   **********^ privatefly.com at Alexa

119.   **********^ *Sparkes, Matthew (10 January 2014). "Ten places where you can spend your bitcoins in the UK". The Telegraph. London. Retrieved 10 September 2013.*

120.   **********^ virgingalactic at Alexa

121.   **********^ *Holpuch, Amanda (22 November 2013). "Virgin Galactic to accept Bitcoin for space flights". The Guardian. Retrieved 24 November 2013.*

122.   **********^ dynamite at Alexa

123.   **********^ *Mat 'Inferiorego' Elfring (17 September 2014). "Dynamite Digital Adds Bitcoin Payment Option and Offers Discount Bundle". CBS Interactive. Retrieved 27 December 2014.*

124.   **********^ clearlycanadian at Alexa

125.   **********^ *"Clearly Canadian Joins Bitcoin Community". finance.yahoo.com. Yahoo! Finance. 23 December 2013. Retrieved 10 February 2014.*

126.   **********^ *Davidson, Kavitha (16 January 2014). "How Many Bitcoins for a Courtside Seat?". bloomberg.com. Bloomberg LP. Retrieved 20 January 2014.*

127.   **********^ *Cindy Cohn; Peter Eckersley; Rainey Reitman & Seth Schoen (17 May 2013). "EFF Will Accept Bitcoins to Support Digital Liberty". Electronic Frontier Foundation. Retrieved 27 April 2014.*

128.   **********^ *Cassady Sharp (22 September 2014). "Greenpeace now accepting bitcoin donations". Greenpeace. Retrieved 31 October 2014.*

129.   **********^ *Emil Protali*

130.   https://finance.yahoo.com/news/bitcoin-taking-off-chinas-biggest-111400936.html, **1 June 2017**

131.   http://www.cnbc.com/2017/05/31/bitcoin-price-forecast-hit-100000-in-10-years.html

References **Ethereum**

1. ∧ **********:*a b c* *Understanding Ethereum (Report). CoinDesk. 24 June 2016.*

2. **********∧ *ConsenSys (2016-06-23). "Ethereum, Gas, Fuel, & Fees". ConsenSys Media. Retrieved 2017-01-15.*

3. ∧ **********:*a b c d* *Aitken, Roger (23 April 2016). "Digital Gold 'Done Right' With DigixDAO Crypto-Trading On OpenLedger". Forbes. Retrieved 28 April 2016.*

4. ∧ **********:*a b* *van Wirdum, Aaron (19 August 2016). "Ethereum Classic Community Navigates a Distinct Path to the Future". Bitcoin Magazine. Retrieved 15 May 2017.*

5. ∧ **********:*a b* *De Jesus, Cecille (19 July 2016). "The DAO Heist Undone: 97% of ETH Holders Vote for the Hard Fork". Futurism, LLC. Retrieved 16 May 2017.*

6. ∧ **********:*a b* *Quentson, Andrew (17 July 2016). "Miners Vote Overwhelmingly in Support of Ethereum's Hardfork". Cryptocoinnews. Retrieved 14 May 2017.*

7. ∧ **********:*a b c* *Buterin, Vitalik (26 July 2016). "Onward from the Hard Fork". Ethereum Foundation. Retrieved 14 May 2017.*

8. ∧ **********:*a b* *Bradley, Miles (17 November 2016). "CoinDesk Research: Ethereum Hard Fork Had Little Impact on Sentiment". Coindesk. Retrieved 14 May 2017.*

9. ∧ **********:*a b c d* Nathaniel Popper for the New York Times. March 27, 2016 Ethereum, a Virtual Currency, Enables Transactions That Rival Bitcoin's

10. ∧ **********:*a b* *Price, Rob (17 June 2016). "Digital Currency Ethereum is Cratering Amid Claims of a $50 Million Hack". Business Insider. Business Insider. Retrieved 14 May 2017.*

11. **Jump up∧** *"What is Ethereum? — Ethereum Homestead 0.1 documentation". ethdocs.org.*

References **Ripple**

1. ∧ **********:*a b c* *"Official source code". Github. Retrieved May 14, 2014.*

2.   ∧ **********:ᵃ ᵇ ᶜ ᵈ ᵉ *Buterin, Vitalik (September 26, 2013). "Ripple is officially open source". Bitcoin Magazine. Coin Publishing Ltd. Retrieved January 25, 2014.*

3.   ∧ **********:ᵃ ᵇ ᶜ ᵈ *"Two US banks are ready to embrace the Ripple protocol". Gigaom. September 24, 2014. Retrieved 2015-06-09.*

4.   **Jump up**∧ *"Ripple Labs Banks $3.5M for Open-Source Payments System and Virtual Currency". Dow Jones & Company. Retrieved January 28, 2014.*

5.   ∧ **********:ᵃ ᵇ *Bradbury, Danny (May 27, 2013). "Chris Larsen: Ripple is HTTP for money". CoinDesk. Coindesk Ltd. Retrieved January 26, 2014.*

6.   ∧ **********:ᵃ ᵇ *"Tech Showcase: Ripple Labs". Institute of International Finance.*

7.   ∧ **********:ᵃ ᵇ ᶜ ᵈ ᵉ *Liu, Alec. "Beyond Bitcoin: a Guide to the Most Promising Cryptocurrencies". Motherboard (beta) blogs. Vice Media Inc.*

8.   ∧ **********:ᵃ ᵇ ᶜ ᵈ *"Safety, liveness and fault tolerance—the consensus choices".*

9.   ∧ **********:ᵃ ᵇ ᶜ *"Stellar Network Fork Prompts Concerns Over Ripple Consensus Protocol".*

10.   **Jump up**∧ *"Crypto-Currency Market Capitalizations". coinmarketcap.com. Retrieved 2014-01-19.*

11.   **Jump up**∧ *"LTC/USD alltime - Bitcoin / Altcoin market overview". cryptocoincharts.info. Retrieved 2014-10-01.*

12.   **Jump up**∧ *Simonite, Tom (2013-04-15). "Bitcoin isn't the only cryptocurrency in town". MIT Technology Review. Retrieved April 24, 2013.*

13.   **Jump up**∧ LTCUSD alltime Litecoin US Dollar chart from BTC-e(cryptocoincharts.info)

14.   **Jump up**∧ *Powers, Shawn (March 2012). "Cryptocurrency: Your total cost is 01001010010" (PDF). Linux Journal (215): 28–29. Retrieved October 21, 2012.*

15.   **Jump up**∧ *BATR (2013-04-17). "Bitcoins risk reward". The Market Oracle. Retrieved April 24, 2013.*

16. ^ **********:a b *Popper, Nathaniel. "The rush to coin virtual money with real value".* The New York Times. The New York Times Company. Retrieved January 26, 2014.

17. ^ **********:a b *Todd, Sarah (April 7, 2015). "Banks Can Cherry-Pick the Best Bits from Bitcoin: Report".* American Banker. Retrieved 2015-06-16.

18. ^ **********:a b c d e *Buterin, Vitalik (February 26, 2013). "Introducing Ripple".* Bitcoin Magazine. Retrieved February 6, 2014.

19. **Jump up^** *Deng, Xiaotie; Graham, Fan Chung, eds. (November 29, 2007). Internet and Network Economics: Third International Workshop, WINE 2007, Proceedings. Germany: Springer. p. 268. ISBN 978-3-540-77104-3.*

20. ^ **********:a b c d *Peck, Morgan (January 14, 2013). "Ripple Could Help or Harm Bitcoin".* IEEE Spectrum. Institute of Electrical and Electronics Engineers. Retrieved January 27, 2014.

21. ^ **********:a b c d e f *Reutzel, Bailey. "Disruptor Chris Larsen Returns with a Bitcoin-Like Payments System".* PaymentSource. Retrieved 18 March 2014.

22. **Jump up^** *Liu, Alec. "Ripple Could Make Bitcoin Great (or Destroy It)".* Motherboard. Retrieved January 27, 2014.

23. ^ **********:a b c *Grant, Rebecca (April 11, 2013). "OpenCoin raises seed round so 'anyone in the world can trade any amount of money in any currency'".* VentureBeat. Retrieved February 6, 2014.

24. **Jump up^** *Craig, Michael (February 5, 2015). "The Race to Replace Bitcoin".* Observer. Retrieved 2015-06-13.

25. ^ **********:a b *"Company Overview of Ripple Labs Inc.".* Bloomberg. Retrieved January 27, 2014.

26. ^ **********:a b c d e *Andrews, Edmund L. (September 24, 2013). "Chris Larsen: Money Without Borders".* Stanford Graduate School of Business. Retrieved 2015-04-10.

27. **Jump up^** *Bala, Dr. Venkatesh (October 8, 2014). "Lessons in Innovation Leadership: Chris Larsen".* Nielsen. The Cambridge Group. Retrieved 2015-06-10.

28. ^ **********:a b c *Perry, John-David (December 5, 2014). "The Future for Global Value Transfers".* Fox Business. Retrieved 2015-06-16.

29.   **Jump up^** *Lashinsky, Adam (August 22, 2014). "Isn't one Internet enough?". Fortune Magazine. Retrieved 2015-04-10.*

30.   **Jump up^** *Shirley, Siluk. "Google Ventures invests in Bitcoin competitor OpenCoin". CoinDesk. Retrieved 18 March 2014.*

31.   ^ **********:a b c d *"FinCEN Fines Ripple Labs Inc. in First Civil Enforcement"(PDF).*

32.   **Jump up^** *"OpenCoin Extends Ripple Network to Include All Bitcoin Merchants and Users". Yahoo Finance. Retrieved 18 March 2014.*

33.   ^ **********:a b *David, Gilson. "OpenCoin: Ripple users can send payments to bitcoin addresses". CoinDesk. Retrieved March 17, 2014.*

34.   **Jump up^** *Kharif, Olga. "Ripple Takes on Western Union With Deal to Grow Payments". Bloomberg. Retrieved January 28, 2014.*

35.   **Jump up^** *"The Future of Money and Bitcoin by Chris Larsen, CEO of OpenCoin". Retrieved February 24, 2015.*

36.   ^ **********:a b *Cooper, Jane (March 11, 2014). "Ripple Labs CEO looks to revolutionise online payments". The Banker. Retrieved 2015-04-10.*

37.   ^ **********:a b c *Ryan, Philip (April 29, 2015). "Western Union Will Give Ripple a Chance". Bank Innovation. Retrieved 2015-06-09.*

38.   ^ **********:a b *Bradbury, Danny. "Ripple Courts Developers, Entrepreneurs With New Initiatives". CoinDesk. Retrieved 18 March 2014.*

39.   **Jump up^** *"Introducing Ripple Client: the iOS App". Ripple blog. Ripple Labs Inc.*

40.   **Jump up^** *Kirk, Jeremy. "Apple removes Blockchain, last Bitcoin wallet app, from iOS App Store". PCWorld. Retrieved 18 March 2014.*

41.   **Jump up^** Download the Ripple Client - Official site Archived June 4, 2015, at the Wayback Machine.

42.   **Jump up^** *Cawrey, Daniel (July 21, 2014). "Ripple Labs Unveils Proposal for New Smart Contract System". coindesk. Retrieved 2015-06-09.*

43. **Jump up^** *Scully, Matt (September 24, 2014). "Alternative Money Mover Ripple Labs Enters U.S. Banking System". American Banker. Retrieved 2015-06-16.*

44. ^ **********:*a b* *Bannister, David (September 30, 2014). "Next out of the block". Banking Technology. Retrieved 2015-06-09.*

45. ^ **********:*a b* *Paul Vigna, Michael Casey (December 4, 2014). "BitBeat: Ripple Partners With Global Payments Service Earthport". Wall Street Journal. Retrieved 2015-06-09.*

46. **Jump up^** *Wilmoth, Josiah (December 13, 2014). "XRP price rise gives Ripple $500 million market cap". CryptoCoinNews. Retrieved 2015-06-09.*

47. **Jump up^** *Reutzel, Bailey (February 23, 2015). "Digital-Only German Bank to Enter U.S. Market, Court Millennials". American Banker. Retrieved 2015-06-09.*

48. ^ **********:*a b* *Riley, Duncan (June 1, 2015). "CBA signs deal with Ripple for Blockchain settlements, may eventually support Bitcoin". Silicon Angle. Retrieved 2015-06-09.*

49. **Jump up^** *Merrett, Rebecca (May 27, 2015). "Commonwealth Bank to launch Ripple payments between its subsidiaries". CIO. Retrieved 2015-06-05.*

50. **Jump up^** *Higgins, Stan (November 3, 2014). "Money20/20 Day 1: Regulators, Finance Giants Forecast Bitcoin's Future". CoinDesk. Retrieved 2015-06-09.*

51. ^ **********:*a b* *"What Ripple's Fincen Fine Means for the Digital Currency Industry". American Banker. May 6, 2015. Retrieved 2015-06-09.*

52. **Jump up^** *"Ripple Labs Expands to Asia Pacific to Serve Regional Demand for Ripple's Real-Time Settlement Protocol". Retrieved June 10, 2016.*

53. **Jump up^** *"Ripple opens London office to serve European demand". Retrieved June 10, 2016.*

54. **Jump up^** *"Ripple Continues Global Growth with New Luxembourg Office to Support Protocol Neutrality". Retrieved June 20, 2016.*

55. **Jump up^** http://www.coindesk.com/global-banks-blockchain-payments-network/

56. **Jump up^** *"Payments platform Ripple inks deal with Accenture". Retrieved June 30, 2016.*

57. ^ **************:ᵃ ᵇ ᶜ ᵈ ᵉ ᶠ ᵍ ʰ ⁱ ʲ *"Blockchain payments firm Ripple signs up 10 more banks and PSPs". Retrieved April 26, 2017.*

58. ^ **************:ᵃ ᵇ ᶜ ᵈ ᵉ ᶠ *"Seven Leading Banks Join Ripple's Global Network". Retrieved June 24, 2016.*

59. ^ **************:ᵃ ᵇ ᶜ ᵈ ᵉ ᶠ *"Several Global Banks Join Ripple's Growing Network". Retrieved September 15, 2016.*

60. **Jump up^** *"CGI adds Ripple gateway to payments portfolio". Retrieved June 10, 2016.*

References **NEM**

1. **Jump up^** *Beikverdi, Alireza. "NEM Launches, Targets Old Economy with Proof-of-Importance". Coin Telegraph. Coin Telegraph. Retrieved 1 April 2015.*

2. **Jump up^** *"GitHub - New Economy Movement". GitHub. Retrieved 4 January 2015.*

3. ^ **************:ᵃ ᵇ *"Tech Bureau partners up with NEM for new blockchain engine". The Merkle. Retrieved 2017-03-23.*

4. **Jump up^** *"How Japanese Blockchain Technology Revolutionizes Municipal Government in Belgium". CoinTelegraph. Retrieved 2017-03-23.*

5. **Jump up^** *Maras, Elliot. "Japanese Financial Institutions Partner With Technology Startups To Utilize The Blockchain". CryptoCoinsNews. Retrieved 21 December 2015.*

6. **Jump up^** *"Top Ten Cryptocurrency NEM Catches on in Japan - CryptoCoinsNews". CryptoCoinsNews. 2016-11-24. Retrieved 2017-03-23.*

7. **Jump up^** *Warner, Matthew. "ChronoBank partners with NEM to create ChronoNEM wallet – allcoinsnews.com". Retrieved 2017-03-23.*

8. **Jump up^** *Mikha, Sean. "How I Got $1500 for Commenting On an Article". Lets Talk Bitcoin. Retrieved 4 January 2015.*

9. **Jump up^** *"A Major Announcement". blog.nem.io. Retrieved 2017-03-11.*

10. **Jump up^** *Tanzarian, Armand. "An Introduction to the New Economy Movement". Cointelegraph. Retrieved 4 January 2015.*

References **Ethereum Classic**

1. **Jump up^** *Ehsani, Farzam (22 December 2016). "Blockchain in Finance: From Buzzword to Watchword in 2016". CoinDesk (News). Retrieved 22 December 2016.*

2. **Jump up^** *Vigna, Paul (28 October 2015). "BitBeat: Microsoft to Offer Ethereum-Based Services on Azure". The Wall Street Journal (Blog). News Corp. Retrieved 17 February 2016.*

3. **Jump up^** *"Account Types, Gas, and Transactions — Ethereum Homestead 0.1 documentation". ethdocs.org. Retrieved 2017-01-15.*

4. **Jump up^** *Ethereum. "Gas and transaction costs | Ethereum Frontier Guide". ethereum.gitbooks.io. Retrieved 2017-01-15.*

5. **Jump up^** *"What is the "Gas" in Ethereum?". CryptoCompare. Retrieved 2017-01-15.*

6. **Jump up^** *ConsenSys (2016-06-23). "Ethereum, Gas, Fuel, & Fees". ConsenSys Media. Retrieved 2017-01-15.*

7. ^ **********⋅ᵃ ᵇ** *"U.S. investment firm launches $10 mln ethereum classic private fund". Reuters. 2017-04-26. Retrieved 2017-04-27.*

8. **Jump up^** *"Ethereum Classic (ETC) price, charts, market cap, and other metrics - CryptoCurrency Market Capitalizations".*

9. **Jump up^** *Adinolfi, Joseph. "Exclusive: Grayscale launches digital-currency fund backed by Silver Lake's co-founder Hutchins". MarketWatch. Retrieved 2017-04-27.*

10. **Jump up^** *Wirdum, Aaron van. "Rejecting Today's Hard Fork, the Ethereum Classic Project Continues on the Original Chain: Here's Why". Bitcoin Magazine. Retrieved 2017-04-27.*

11. **Jump up^**https://ethereumclassic.github.io/assets/ETC_Declaration_of_Independence.pdf

12. **Jump up^** *Coppola, Frances. "Ethereum: The Battle Of The Chains". Forbes. Retrieved 2017-04-27.*

13.   **Jump up^** Dabek, Daniel (29 Jul 2016). *"Ethereum Classic Brings War To The Cryptocurrency Exchanges". CoinIdol. Retrieved 29 Jul 2016.*

14.   **Jump up^** Vigna, Paul (1 August 2016). *"The Great Digital-Currency Debate: 'New' Ethereum Vs. Ethereum 'Classic'". The Wall Street Journal: Moneybeat. Retrieved 4 August 2016.*

www.ingramcontent.com/pod-product-compliance
Lightning Source LLC
Chambersburg PA
CBHW072040190526
45165CB00018B/1185